To Mary Olive,
Swim fast with the Dolphins

Marvin Schwartz

Racing Starts

Racing Starts
A History of Competitive Swimming in Central Arkansas

Marvin Schwartz

Copyright 2011 by Marvin Schwartz.
All rights reserved. No part of this book may be reproduced in any form, except for brief passages quoted within reviews, without the express written consent of the author.

Marvin Schwartz
11 Racquet Court
Little Rock, AR 72227
501.312.2288
schwartz921@comcast.net

ISBN: 978-0-9838992-0-4

Design: H. K. Stewart

Front cover photo: *Little Rock's Neka Mabry (in the white Georgia cap) has the advantage of a quick start in the 50-meter race at the International Swimming Hall of Fame Pool, Fort Lauderdale, Florida, 2002.*

Back cover photo: *Dolphin swimmer Lexi Rasnic of Hot Springs*

Printed in the United States of America
This book is printed on archival-quality paper that meets requirements of the American National Standard for Information Sciences, Permanence of Paper, Printed Library Materials, ANSI Z39.48-1984.

This book is dedicated to the thousands of Arkansas swimmers known only in their local communities, who were part of something larger than themselves, and who gave all of themselves to be a part of it. Though they rarely stood on the victory podium or won media acclaim, they, too, were champions.

Champs—YWCA swimmers demonstrate form that won the 8-year-old and under division at the Shreveport Invitational Swimming and Diving Meet last week. The girls are (from left) Jane Thomas, Sandy Burris, Ferris Cook, Diane Letzig, and Brenda Grimes.
Photo and caption: *Arkansas Democrat,* **July 7, 1963**

Contents

Acknowledgements 9

Preface 11

Introduction 13

Chapter 1. 1920s Through 1940s 17

Chapter 2. 1950s 31

Chapter 3. 1960s 39

Chapter 4. Little Rock Racquet Club 49

Chapter 5. 1970s 55

Chapter 6. The Winning Formula: Parents 67

Chapter 7. 1980s 71

Chapter 8. 1990s 87

Chapter 9. The Winning Formula: Motivation 97

Chapter 10. 2000s 103

Chapter 11. To An Athlete Dying Young 111

Chapter 12. Arkansas Masters Swimming 113

Chapter 13. The Winning Formula: Life Impact 119

Chapter 14. Afterword 123

Appendices 127
   Appendix A: Swim Teams and Head Coaches 127
   Appendix B: Arkansans in 1969 National Age Group Top 5 Ranking 128
   Appendix C: Arkansas Swimming Hall of Fame 130
   Appendix D: Dolphins Achievements 131

Index 135

About the Author 141

ACKNOWLEDGEMENTS

The author is greatly appreciative of the many swimmers, swim parents, and coaches interviewed for this book. In addition, the following persons and organizations generously shared photographs, scrapbooks, and other materials to assist in compiling this history.

Arkansas Democrat-Gazette
Hannah Bakke
Greg Ballard, Boys and Girls Club of Central Arkansas
Mary Dawn Blair
Patrick Bass, Central Arkansas Swim Club
John Brooks archives, Butler Center, Arkansas Studies Institute, Central Arkansas Library Systems
Mike Booth
Dr. Richard Clark, Pulaski County Historical Society
Randy Ensminger
Roy Gentry
Liz and Terry Genz
Randy Hathaway
Robert Hayden
Mary Lou Jaworski
Dr. Ted Jolly
Dixie Knight Photography
Mary Kok-Brann
Chuck Letzig
Neka Mabry
James Martin, Project Intern
Doug Martin
Tedd Maxfield, YMCA of Metropolitan Little Rock
Keith McAfee
Kathy McAlister
Mike Neuhofel
Bob Ocken Photography

Kees Oudegeest
Pat Riley, Sr.
SWIM Magazine
Tay Stratton
Sammy Turner
Manuel and Gwen Twillie
Benny Wise

Preface

This book focuses on swimmers and athletic programs in central Arkansas. Team documentation and media reporting of swimming, however, have been inconsistent over the years. In researching this history, every effort has been made to build a comprehensive record of achievement. The author asks for readers' pardon if inaccuracies or omissions are found in this first-ever compilation of Arkansas swimming.

In addition, a much larger story and rich history remains to be told of swimming teams across all of Arkansas. Long-established swimming programs in Jonesboro, Fort Smith, Conway, and other communities continue to help generations of young people develop keen minds and healthy bodies. Inside the YMCAs and Boys Clubs of many Arkansas towns, swimmers and their coaches are continuing that tradition, and untold numbers of Arkansas families have been and continue to be the beneficiaries.

Two groups of swimmers with significant accomplishments are not included because their stories could not be fully presented in the scope of this work. They are Arkansas swimmers with disabilities—athletes who compete in Special Olympics and Para Olympics programs—and the Arkansas swimmers who compete in the state Senior Olympics. Each group has recorded remarkable achievements and produced champions of the highest order.

Rough water at the Little Rock YWCA didn't dampen the enthusiasm of Wendy Rynning (rear left), Karen Gore (rear right), and Barbara Hicks (diving) in 1970. The basement 20-yard pool hosted hundreds of swimmers for crowded, noisy swim meets. Coach Mary Lou Jaworski's office was behind the wire fencing in the rear.

INTRODUCTION

When did competitive swimming begin in central Arkansas?

Perhaps it was the first time a couple of game young men were dangling their feet over the edge of a dock and a pretty girl in a bathing suit walked by. We've been off to the races ever since.

We are, by nature, competitive creatures. And if honor or more tangible rewards can be won, a starter's gun and the resulting adrenalin rush may produce record achievements.

Arkansas' earliest swimming races—YMCA programs dating back to the 1920s—gave little indication that national and world-ranked athletes would one day emerge from Little Rock pools. There would also be dynamic swimming coaches who built top age group programs here.

The first of these was Jimmy Miller, whose Little Rock Boys Club teams in the 1950s and 1960s had some of the fastest 10 & Under boys in the nation. In the 1980s and 1990s, Paul Blair, coach of the Little Rock Dolphins Swim Team, gained renown as a sprint coach and his teams achieved national prominence unprecedented in this state.

But there were many others—men and women, coaches and athletes—who loved the sport and nurtured its growth in the early years. From the 1950s onward, as

> We are, by nature, competitive creatures. And if honor or more tangible rewards can be won, a starter's gun and the resulting adrenalin rush may produce record achievements.

1925 Little Rock YMCA State Champion Swim Team

Pulchritude for Swim Meet
This bevy of beauties will represent the Little Rock Boys Club at the state AAU swimming and diving meet here this week. Left to right, they are: Debby Nelson, Pat Maddox, Helen Keith, Sandra Wafer, Sara Wafer, Marybeth Wafer and Julie Owen. The diving chores will be capably handled by the Misses Nelson, Maddox, and Owen.
Photo and caption: *Arkansas Democrat, 1952*

swimming across the US gained popularity, a group of Arkansas pioneers became advocates for swimming. They understood how valuable an athletic program would be if it bonded children, families, and communities in a common effort.

> *"No one loved swimming more or for better reasons than the people of Arkansas. For the amount of people that swim there, it is amazing how many Arkansans have been nationally ranked."*
> Harvey Humphries

Flip turns and goggles

Competitive swimming has changed dramatically over the years.

In Little Rock, this history begins in the 1920s with neighborhood kids who trained in Boys Club and YMCA basement 20-yard pools. By the 1960s, that venue had been replaced by modern 25-yard and 50-meter pools.

The flip turn was introduced at the 1956 Olympics at Melbourne, about the same time the modern butterfly stroke was introduced. Goggles were first used in the 1976 Games at Montreal. Boxer style swim trunks popular in the 1940s were replaced by nylon suits in the 1950s. Today, they are known as "drag suits" and worn only for loose fitting comfort during workouts. Nylon racing suits have gotten smaller and tighter over the years as designers gained better understanding of hydrodynamics. And full body suits, those engineered marvels of water-repellent synthetic material, are now banned from sanctioned competition, having contributed to an alarming rewrite of world records.

Underwater swimming using a streamline dolphin kick is astonishingly efficient, possibly faster than any stroke swum on the surface of the water. Restrictions now prohibit swimmers from completing full pool lengths below the surface and rising for breath only at turns.

But technical innovation has not changed the essential character of the sport.

Amid the crowd of swimmers and coaches on deck at an age group swim meet, screaming parents still shriek their hysterical support to six and eight-year olds whose heads are barely large enough to fill a latex swim cap.

Lean and muscular adolescents still shake out their long limbs before a race, then launch themselves off starting blocks with astonishing reflex and speed.

And age group champions continue to emerge from ordinary homes, achieving personal best times much to the amazement of parents and swimmers alike. Those breakthroughs are less of a surprise to coaches, who repeatedly remind their swimmers of the direct payoff of personal effort, who track their races and their daily yardage with stop watch in hand, who

stand on deck amidst the screaming crowds to offer post-race hugs of consolation or high fives of acclaim to their young team members.

High energy scenarios

These high energy scenarios are happening most every weekend at YMCA, college, private club, and municipal pools across Arkansas. Yet little attention is paid by local and state media. High school swimming exists in Arkansas, but it is hardly a glamour sport that draws cheerleaders and Friday night crowds.

Some may find it odd that in a landlocked state dominated by football and farming the demanding sport of swimming has gained such passionate participation.

To understand the sport and its compelling appeal to children and families—many believe it to be the most perfect training for injury-free physical development—one needs to consider a number of complex factors.

Start with talent. A young person must have or develop an affinity for the water, a comfort level sustained through two or more hours per day of aerobic and hypoxic levels of stress. Add to that a mastery of stroke technique. Mix in an uncommon degree of personal drive and willingness to balance swimming with school work and social engagements.

If success is to be gained, however, this aspiring swimmer needs much more. Parents must chauffeur their son or daughter to daily swim practice, must be willing

> Some may find it odd that in a landlocked state dominated by football and farming the demanding sport of swimming has gained such passionate participation.

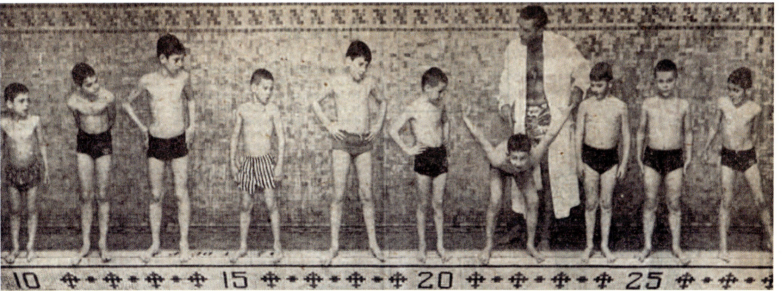

Jimmy Miller at the Little Rock Boys Club

INTRODUCTION 15

This is the paradox of Arkansas swimming, that a most solitary endeavor requires comprehensive and committed family and community support.

Paul Blair at the Little Rock Racquet Club

to compromise their personal schedules and their family finances to weekend out-of-town or out-of-state travel. Competitive swimmers must have daily or twice daily access to a swimming pool of proper length, with lanes separate from water aerobic classes or recreational usage. And no team will succeed without a dedicated coach.

This is the paradox of Arkansas swimming—that a most solitary endeavor requires comprehensive and committed family and community support.

The payoff

What is the payoff, therefore, from the dedication to the sport expressed by every coach and athlete?

College scholarships are available for the most talented, and more assistance is now available for women swimmers than in previous years. But financial support for men's college swimming has declined. Extended fame or fortune await only the fortunate few. Even the Arkansas Swimming Hall of Fame, that worthy endeavor to honor the sport's local champions, recognizes only a few persons each year.

If the swimmers interviewed for this book could speak in a single voice, their testimony might be:

Because of my team, my coach, and a hard-earned process of self discovery, swimming gave me challenges to overcome, gave me the skills and prowess to set and exceed my own goals. It gave me the strength of character to know all I was capable of as an individual and a team member. And it brought me within the influence of those who saw more in me than I had ever presumed to possess.

Swimming gave me the rites of passage to the values I carry today. And in those splendid, transient years when I moved with grace and power in a weightless ballet, in that most demanding and unnatural element, I found and defined myself.

I swam because I loved it.

Chapter 1. 1920s Through 1940s

Naturally Talented Swimmers Emerge
Arkansas competitive swimming began in recreational pools and learn-to-swim programs. Public organizations such as the YMCA and the Boys Club offered the earliest facilities and structure. With little formal support or training, a generation of naturally talented swimmers emerged.

Millwood Pool

Informal swimming races were part of the fun in the 1920s at Little Rock's earliest water parks, Millwood Pool and Willow Springs, spring-fed facilities on the outskirts of the city. But Millwood also contributed to competitive swimming. The pool's summer day camp was operated by Billy Kramer, who taught swimming there. The Kramer daughters became notable athletes in the 1940s—Rosalind as a swimmer and Ruth as a diver.

In July 1940, Millwood Pool hosted the annual Arkansas AAU swimming competition. The program included an "Aquacade" with water ballet and lifesaving demonstrations. Proceeds from the event sent Arkansas swimmers to national AAU meets.

Millwood Pool was the site of the original performances of the "fire dive." The flamboyant ritual is credited to Millwood owner Pat Storey who doused his long underwear with gasoline, ignited himself, then spectacularly dove into the pool, already aflame with gasoline. For the next

Standing Tall. *Lifeguards Raymond Scott (left) and Hamilton Gunn were icons of trust in this 1932 photo. White City Pool guards had to be particularly careful of swimmers who went past the red rail and stepped off into deep water. Guards assigned to the pool sun deck would lower a bucket to bring water up to cool their station. The shaded area below the seated life guard was popular for couples.*

Opening Day at White City Pool, June 16, 1922
Little Rock's municipal pool drew large crowds during its summer seasons. The city street car line ended on Kavanaugh Boulevard near the gates to the pool, and families came with their lunch baskets to spend full days at the one million-gallon capacity pool. When White City Pool closed in 1939, the Little Rock Recreation Commission reported that the pool had been used by approximately 50,000 people each summer, some 20,000 free admissions had been given annually to children from character-building organizations, approximately 500 children had been taught to swim free each year, and free lifesaving classes offered. The pool area, once known as Forest Park, is in today's Heights neighborhood.

thirty years, this daredevil showmanship was performed by divers at Arkansas water carnivals and swimming programs.

White City Pool

Outdoor swimming was immensely popular at Little Rock's White City Pool, which operated from 1922 until 1939 in an area originally known as Forest Park and today known as the Heights. The pool and surrounding area were called White City because of the profusion of new electric lights in the entertainment section of the park.

On August 25, 1932, White City Pool hosted Arkansas' first outdoor AAU-sanctioned swimming and diving competition.

Ready for Racing. *The 1st Arkansas AAU Swimming and Diving Meet was hosted at White City Pool on August 25, 1932. By this time, the central wooden corral, part of the original design, had been removed. Temporary bleachers were constructed above the wading area, and racing lanes were strung across the pool's midsection.*

Swimmers came from Jonesboro, Conway, Lake Village, Searcy, Warren, Hot Springs, Fort Smith, Russellville, Little Rock, and North Little Rock. Personal competition between members of the Little Rock YMCA and the White City swim teams was a crowd favorite, as were the high diving competitions.

"The excellent facilities of your pool…made the meet the best possible. I believe that this will be the foundation of a wonderful future for swimming in Arkansas."
August 26, 1932 letter from Alvin Bell, a member of the local AAU Committee, to Leroy Scott, White City Pool Manager

Despite its popularity and high summer attendance, pool design and high maintenance costs made White City Pool a financial drain on the city.

Fair Park and War Memorial Pool

A new municipal pool was opened in 1942 in a central section of Little Rock known as Fair Park. Fair Park Pool had platform diving and a deep diving well that converted to a 25-meter racing venue. A multi-use pool, Fair Park also had wading and recreational swim areas. On Sunday afternoons, some of the more daring young men would do clown dives. War Memorial Pool, like White City before it, was a crowded and fun place during hot Little Rock summers.

Fair Park Pool, *1942, photographed from the top of the park's Ferris Wheel. Racing at the pool was conducted in the diving area on the left.*

Several thousand Little Rock bathers attended the opening of the new Fair Park Pool on May 9, 1942. Built as a federal WPA project at a cost of $103,000, it replaced the White City Pool, which had closed two years earlier.

Little Rock divers entertained the summer crowds at Fair Park Pool, and Pfeiffer's Department Store presented its annual Bathing Beauty Review and style show, complete with Hawaiian music, song and dance. A water ballet performed by local girls accompanied many of the competitions.

Evening programs at the pool ended in the immensely popular Fire Dive. His clothing doused with gasoline, a plucky young man would be set aflame on the high platform. Gasoline on the water surface ignited when the diver entered, adding to the spectacle.

"Y" Swimming Team Wins Two State Titles

5th Consecutive Year for State Champions

The YMCA senior swimming team added two new crowns to its list the past week. Monday, the team copped the state "Y" championship, outswimming all other contestants in a meet staged at the Warren YMCA. Friday night, the team swept through to a victory at the Little Rock Boys Club AAU tournament. The win at the state "Y" meet was the fifth consecutive year that the local organization has taken this title. The "Y" preps and juniors teams also won in their divisions in the AAU meet, the three teams scoring a combined total of 257 points as compared to 152 for their top opponent.

Members of the senior team are, left to right: Paul Gruenberg, captain; Robinson Campbell, Bill Moose, Charles Driver, Allan Withee, and Ott C. Stahl, chairman of the "Y" swimming committee. Team members not pictured are: Sherman Thomas, Oliver Brockman, and J.D. Rheinhart.

Photo and Caption: September 13, 1931

In 1947, the site hosted the Men's National Juniors Outdoor 3-Meter AAU Diving Championships. Edward Kennedy, Secretary of the U.S. Olympic Committee and a referee and judge of the diving, was impressed with the facilities. He suggested Fair Park Pool apply to host the next Olympic trials.

The pool and surrounding park area was renamed War Memorial in the early 1950s. The Fair Park/War Memorial Pool was the leading state venue for outdoor swimming and diving competitions until the 1960s when new 25-yard and 50-meter pools were built in Little Rock.

Early Champions at the YMCA

Downtown Little Rock had three indoor, basement pools within a few blocks of each other. Thousands of local children learned to swim at the Little Rock YMCA, the Little Rock Boys Club, and the Little Rock YWCA.

The YMCA's first downtown building and pool was at 6th and Capitol Street, a structure that now houses the *Arkansas Democrat-Gazette*. A 1925 photo shows a swim team on site with the caption "State Champions." In 1928, the YMCA moved to a new building on Broadway, which also had a basement pool. Through the 1930s and early 1940s, the Little Rock YMCA team was the consistent winner in Arkansas swimming meets. A news article in 1931 stated that YMCA swimmers were

Fair Park Beauties—*This bevy of pulchritudinous swimmers will perform in a colorful water ballet as a feature attraction of the men's national junior diving championships at Fair Park Pool July 28. From the left to right, the girls are: Dorothy Dill, Sue Keith, Flora Carson, Charlotte Simmen and Zelma Kenchilo.*

Photo and Caption: Arkansas Democrat, July 26, 1947

"Fire Diver" *Hardie Thomas performs at the 1947 program.*

the overall winners and "most accomplished" in the first state-wide AAU meet.

In the mid-1930s, top swimmers for the Little Rock YMCA included Billy Gruenberg and L. B. Parker. Parker would become one of the first swimming coaches at the Little Rock Boys Club. In a 1935 competition in front of 3,000 local spectators, YMCA swimmers—Billy and Paul Gruenberg, Elbert Wilkes, and Alston Jennings—set a state record of 1:15 in the 160-Yard Freestyle Relay.

A New Start at the Boys Club

The Little Rock Boys Club was established in 1913 and operated out of downtown churches and office buildings. In 1924, local donors raised funds to purchase and renovate a large facility on 8th and Scott Street. The building was destroyed in a 1929 fire.

At the time of the fire, the Boys Club had more than 1,600 memberships, and its leadership, Executive Director Thomas Craighead and his successor Billy Mitchell, had the respect of the community.

Construction costs for a replacement building were estimated at $150,000. These funds had to be raised locally in a very challenging time. Only two months had passed since the 1929 stock market crash. In the near future, banks and employers in Little Rock would be closing their doors with the onset of the Great Depression.

In this gloomy economic environment, the Little Rock Boys Club leadership announced its capital campaign. The community responded, and $150,000 was raised in less than two weeks.

Mitchell contacted his former boss, Craighead, now the director of the new and modern Flatbush Boys Club in Brooklyn, New York. Building plans and club designs from Flatbush and other leading Boys Clubs were used to rebuild the Little Rock facility. Modern Boys Clubs across the nation had basement

Program cover from the 21st Annual Arkansas Championship in 1952. State championship outdoor meets were first held at White City Pool in 1931.

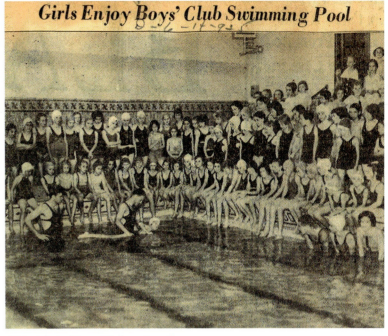

600 girls in Boys Club swim classes
Recruitment for the boys and girls swimming teams took place at learn-to-swim sessions. Free swimming classes at the Boys Club and White City pools brought promising girls to the attention of swim coach and former star athlete Bess Butler.
Arkansas Gazette, *June 14, 1935*

In the 1930s, the Boys Club conducted 'postal swims' in conjunction with other clubs around the country, sending in time trial results for a national contest. Marathon swims were also recorded, with boys and girls completing the lap equivalent of a swim from Little Rock to Chicago or Miami.

Are Swimmers Smarter Than Other Athletes?
"Swimming teaches you to work hard. It sets the path to gain knowledge and be disciplined and dedicated about it."
Amy Gruber Burgess

The first races were held at the Boys Club pool on June 31, 1931, with young swimmers rated as midgets (10 and under), juniors, intermediates, and seniors. The races were from 10 to 40-yard events, including some underwater.

20 Yards and 4 Lanes

The Little Rock Boys Club Pool was one of three 20-yard pools in downtown Little Rock in the 1930s.

The first races were held at the Boys Club pool on June 31, 1931, with young swimmers rated as midgets (10 and under), juniors, intermediates, and seniors. The races were from 10 to 40-yard events, including some underwater. More meets followed on a weekly basis, and the results were reported in the newspapers. Swimming, the newspapers wrote, was the most popular sport at the new club that summer.

In a 1933 newspaper article, Executive Director Billy Mitchell said he counted some 500 bodies in the pool and stated, "at times, it was possible to walk across the pool on top of the swimmers' heads."

What Is the Difference Between Sprinters and Distance Swimmers?
"Sprinters are more proud of themselves than distance swimmers. They feel superior."
Mickey Gunn

Arkansas swimming power team of the 1940s.
This formidable lineup at Little Rock Boys Club included two Neil Martin Victory Trophy winners (Carl Quaintance, 1946, and Bobby Branch, 1950) and two Martin award finalists (Mickey Gunn, 1948, and Sue Keith 1946). Jimmy Miller, second from left in middle row, was a swim team member and part-time coach at the Boys Club at the time.

Swimming Champions—Members of the swimming team of the Little Rock Boys Club, winners of all three divisions in the state AAU meet last week, are pictured above. Left to right, they are: Front row—Marvin Corden, Virginia Piper, Rosalind Kramer, Sue Keith, Carolyn Potter, Ruth Kramer, and Coy Burch. Middle row—Bobby Bell, Jimmy Miller, Henry Fitzgibbon, Jack Branch, Frank Thompson, and Luther Young; back row—Bobby Branch, Mickey Gunn, Sonny Hoff, Gene Crawford, Carl Quaintance, and Hardie Thomas.
Photo and Caption: Arkansas Democrat, August 25, 1946

pools. Little Rock got one, too. Identical to the pools at the YMCA and YWCA, the Boys Club pool was 20 yards long and four lanes wide.

In June 1931, the Little Rock Boys Club opened a new building. Above the front entry door, a plaque declared, "Enter, Ye Men of Tomorrow." Free swimming classes were offered, and swim teams soon followed. From the mid-1940s onward, the best Arkansas men and women swimmers and divers, many of them national champions, represented the Boys Club.

Pfeifer Kiwanis Camp

Some outdoor swimming took place at the Pfeifer Kiwanis Camp, an 80-acre site west of Little Rock. Little Rock Kiwanis Club members sold the land to the Boys Club, and in 1920, a summer camp for boys was established on the site. Kiwanis members raised funds for the camp, following the example of Preston Pfeifer, who made a large donation to the fundraising effort in honor of his father, Joseph Pfeifer, a Little Rock pioneer merchant.

The Pfeiffer Kiwanis Camp had a 25-meter pool. In the 1950s, the Camp Director was Jimmy Miller, the former Boys Club swimmer and current swim team coach, who was becoming a major figure in central Arkansas swimming. Miller's swimmers from the Boys Club team worked as camp counselors and taught swimming there.

The Pfeifer Camp included a section of the Little Maumelle River. The shallow river passed under a county bridge whose iron girders had been painted red. Rumors of the "Red Bridge Club" were rampant. Jimmy Miller and his roughneck Little Rock swimming pals were diving off the bridge, back flips and all.

The Little Rock Boys Club junior relay team, *winner of the state AAU title in its event last season and holder of the state record, will defend its title Thursday night in the state swimming meet at White City pool. Left to right: Eugene Reigler, Gilbert Garner, John Signoracci, Elmer Diemer, and Coach J. B. Roberts*
Photo and caption: August 25, 1932

John Brooks recalled the James brothers racing at White City Pool. "The brothers were so fast and so far ahead of everyone else, they would stop at the turn, push their hair back as they let other swimmers catch up, then go on to win the race."

Arkansas' James Brothers
Obell (left) and Odell James, twin brothers, of El Dorado, who hold several swimming records, will represent Lion Oil Sales Company at the annual A.A.U. swim meet at White City tonight. The twins will participate in the 40-yard, 100-yard, and 220-yard and 440-yard free style events. They have just returned from the Southern A.A.U. meet at New Orleans where Obell won first place in a free style event and Odell placed fourth in three events.
Photo and Caption: Arkansas Gazette, August 1, 1935

Perfect form from the board to the water will be the aim of these lads as they seek honors at the National AAU Three-Meter Junior Outdoor Diving Championship at the Fair Park Pool. Starting at lower left, and in clockwise order, they are Sonny Hoff and Hardie Lee Thomas, both of Little Rock; Ray Traindale of Coral Gables, Fla., Barney Cipriani of Detroit, Mich, and Carl Quaintance of Little Rock, state champion.
Photo and caption: Arkansas Gazette, July 28, 1947

Racing in the 1940s

Little Rock Boys Club wins state AAU swim dive champs at Fair Park

"When it comes to producing swimmer and divers—girls or boys—nobody comes close to the Little Rock Boys Club. Last night, teams from the Little Rock organization displayed their superiority by walking off with all three champion ships.....almost a duplicate of their feats in the indoor show staged in Conway last spring."

Arkansas Gazette, August 21, 1946

A few talented swimmers represented YMCAs and military bases across the state, but the majority of Arkansas' best swimmers, men and women, were listed with the Boys Club. Girl swimmers in the headlines were Rosalind Kramer and Sue Keith. Both had been coached by Bess Butler at the Boys Club. The boy's team top swimmers were Mickey Gunn, brothers Jack and Bobby Branch, Gene Crawford, and Tony Koonce. Local divers—Carl Quaintance, Hardie Thomas, and Sonny Hoff—also gained prominence.

John Brooks

In 1933, John Brooks had the best summer job in Little Rock. The 10-year old was on the "free swim" list for kids that did chores at the White City Pool. Brooks was on hand for the first AAU swimming

John Brooks, *1945. As a swim instructor in the U.S. Marines, Brooks introduced training to help soldiers survive sinking ships and beach landings.*

competitions and the White City water carnivals with their famous fire dives.

Brooks has been called one of the founding fathers of Arkansas swimming. He swam for the Little Rock Boys Club in the 1940s. He worked as a coach there and at the Little Rock YMCA. He taught swimming at Fair Park Pool. He built a small outdoor pool in west Little Rock and operated his own swim school. He was a swim parent whose son Clyde ranked as one of the fastest age group swimmers in the nation.

During his military service in the 1940s, Brooks swam for the Marine Corps team and taught swimming at Camp Matthews at San Diego, California. At that time, poorly-prepared soldiers were drowning on reefs in the Pacific when they jumped from their landing crafts into deep water.

"We introduced a new swimming program for drown-proofing soldiers," Brooks said. "We also taught them to jump off a thirty-foot tower to simulate jumping from a hit aircraft carrier. If they would freeze, we'd push them off."

In the 1960s, he established the Brooks Pool Company, which became a leading specialty construction firm in Arkansas. He taught swimming at the Arkansas School for the Blind and was an early advocate for age group competitive swimming. In 1986, Brooks was among the first inductees into the Arkansas Swimming Hall of Fame.

Mickey Gunn

Mickey Gunn at 80 years old is still tall and lanky, with a swimmer's long arm extension. He began setting Arkansas freestyle records as a 14-year old in 1944. Over a seven-year period swimming for the Little Rock Boys Club, Little Rock High School, and Northwest Louisiana State College, he won sixteen state championships and swam on eight championship relay teams. At the time, he held more titles than any other swimmer in the state.

The newspapers called him "Big Mickey Gunn." In 1948, the *Arkansas Gazette* called him "the fastest swimmer in the South." That year, he was a finalist for the Neil Martin Victory Trophy, Arkansas' highest recognition of an amateur athlete.

Mickey Gunn (left) and Jack Branch at Northwestern State College of Louisiana, 1949
Arkansas swimmers in the 1940s attended Northwestern State College of Louisiana (now Northwestern State University) at Natchitoches, Louisiana. The school had a strong swimming program, and the team competed with schools and military bases across the South. Following the competitions, women swimmers performed water ballet. Divers performed clown dives. Despite the prominence of swimming on campus, the school ended its competitive program by 1957.

Articles from *The Current Sauce*, the Northwestern State College campus newspaper, October 1949:

Little Rock makes big splash in Northwestern's Natatorium
   Arkansans flock to Northwestern like Okies to California, but not for the same reason.
   Arkansans on the swimming team: Jack Branch: 100 back; Mickey Gunn: 200 & 400 free; Jack Gaston and Bo Justings, both from El Dorado; Divers: clown divers and gymnasts—Wally Fryer, Jimmy Miller (also swims middle distance), Dick Sisemore. Expected in Spring semester: Tony Koonce, Bernard Waller.
   All these boys got their start in the Little Rock Boys Club and have had a hand in that organization winning the Arkansas State AAU meet every year for the past 15 years. "Figure on having Little Rock's best swimmers coming down here for at least the next 20 years," said Jimmy Miller.
   So you see, Arkansas isn't all Ozarks, Razorbacks, and mountaineer moonshiners.

Five Reasons why we like Little Rock, Arkansas is because of Carl Quaintance, Buddy Countryman, Jack Branch, Wally Fryer, and Mr. and Mrs. Gunn*—Our campus (not to mention our swimming team) is much better off with these citizens.
*Jackie Gunn was on the NLSC women's swim team.

Are Swimmers Smarter than Other Athletes?
"Swimmers are actually smarter *and* stronger. You take a ragtag bunch of kids, bring them together, and they win. It's the kind of a romantic story."
Mickey Gunn

Swimmers and Divers of the 1940s

Tony Koonce *is listed in many news reports in the 1940s, winning individual freestyle sprint events and record-setting relays. He swam for the Little Rock Boys Club and worked as a lifeguard and swim teacher at the Fair Park Pool. Koonce competed for Little Rock Junior College, where he and Harold May were the swim team's student coaches, and he also swam for Northwest Louisiana State. He was a swim coach at the Little Rock YMCA in the 1950s, recruiting local youngsters like future Arkansas Swimming Hall of Famer Tom Roberts.*

Tribute to Carl Quaintance in the program book from the National Junior Outdoor 3-Meter AAU Diving Championships, held at Little Rock, July 1947.

Neil Gibson Martin Victory Trophy
Carl Quaintance
Outstanding Arkansas AAU Athlete for 1946

Quaintance set a precedent for the Arkansas AAU by winning both the boys and men's diving championships at the age of 14. He later attended the University of Texas, and as a freshman diver, captured the Southwest Conference Championship in 1943. He placed first in the Texas-Mexico International meet that same year.

Carl served as swimming instructor with the Navy at Great Lakes, IL and was a member of the station team. During the National AAU meet of 1946, held at the Naval Base at Bainbridge, MD, he placed sixth in the low-board championship.

Last summer, Quaintance represented the Little Rock Boys Club and placed ninth in the National AAU 3-Meter Championship at San Diego, CA. He won both the platform and springboard events during the State AAU meet of 1946.

Swimmers and Divers of the 1940s

Rosalind Kramer was an early star, winning her first race as a 12-year old in 1939. By the mid-1940s, Kramer had become a prodigy of Bess Butler, a former backstroke champion who taught swimming at the LRBC. In 1946, the Boys Club sent Kramer and Butler to Kansas City for a Junior National AAU meet.

"I swam all the freestyle events, 40 yards and up to the mile, and I won all the state meets" Rosalind Kramer Stone said. Contacted at her Massachusetts home in 2010, Rosalind spoke of teaching swimming for more than 50 years. The 83-year old said she had swum some 40 laps in her home pool that very morning.

Gene Crawford was frequently identified in 1940's swimming news reports. At the 1943 state AAU championship meet, he posted a 29.5 in the 50-Meter Freestyle to defeat defending champion Robert Brooke.

Sgt. Robert Brooke was a repeat winner at Arkansas AAU swim championships in 1942-44. Brooke was a state record holder in Pennsylvania and Virginia who swam for Camp Robinson in North Little Rock. He posted Arkansas times of 29.8 in the 50-Meter Freestyle and 1:08 in the 100-Meter Freestyle.

In 1944, the Arkansas Gazette promoted an upcoming state championship swim meet, writing, "Soldier, sailor, and civilian aquatic stars representing four clubs and service bases will compete for honors in the annual Arkansas AAU indoor swimming and diving championships at the Little Rock Boys Club pool."

In addition to Camp Robinson, Army swim teams entered the meet from camps at Monticello, Stuttgart, and Camden.

> "I swam all the freestyle events, 40 yards and up to the mile, and I won all the state meets."
>
> Rosalind Kramer Stone

> "I had never seen a 50-meter pool before," Gunn said. "I learned to swim in the Caddo River, I trained in the Boys Club 20-yard pool, and there I was at this big pool in the hot California sun. My first heat was for the 100 meters. At the turn, I faded."
>
> Mickey Gunn

Gunn got his first airplane ride as a swimmer. In 1946, he flew to San Diego to race in the Senior National AAU Championships. The Boys Club sent him, along with Gene Crawford, and Carl Quaintance. Seating was down the length of the airplane, military style. The Little Rock swimmers landed in Los Angeles and hitchhiked south to the swim meet.

"I had never seen a 50-meter pool before," Gunn said. "I learned to swim in the Caddo River, I trained in the Boys Club 20-yard pool, and there I was at this big pool in the hot California sun. My first heat was for the 100 meters. At the turn, I faded."

Gunn went on to win numerous victories, high point awards, and state certifications as the leading high school swimmer in Arkansas. In 1947, he married his high school sweetheart Jacque Hogan, also a swimmer.

"Swimming was a family that gave us support and love," Jacque said in a 2010 interview. "I was more proud of my Boys Club jacket than any letter sweater from high school."

The Gunns enrolled together at Northwestern Louisiana State College, where Mickey became swim team captain. His last races were in 1947. A career in agriculture and finance followed. Today, the Gunns live in Beebe. They've been married 63 years. Mickey still recalls the positive life-influences that swimming provided him.

Little Rock JC's championship swim team is shown above. The Trojan swimmers won the AIC championship at the Little Rock Boys Club this month and came through the season undefeated. The girls are, left to right, Eleanor Bogart, Sue Keith, Harriet Goldberg, and Peggy Lafferty. The boys are, left to right, Richard Schmidt, Murray Coulter, Charles Green, Coach Harold May, Sam Stiles, Tony Koonce, and R. L. Gentry.
Photo and Caption, Arkansas Gazette, May 17, 1948

"Swimming was an asset to my well being," he said. "It was something I felt good about internally."

Sue Keith Wrape

"Little Sue Keith, Bess Butler's pride and joy, led the field of swimmers, to win four first places. She was top swimmer in the tourney, scoring the most points."
Arkansas Democrat, 1945

Wrape was thirteen-years old when the newspaper reported on that local swim meet. A year earlier, Bess Butler recognized the girl's talent when Wrape was taking Red Cross swimming classes at Fair Park Pool. Butler taught her all three strokes (freestyle, backstroke, and breaststroke) at a time when most swimmers specialized in just one. For the next four years, Wrape was rarely beaten. She was almost always the high point winner.

In 1946, the *Arkansas Gazette* called her "a brilliant star at the Little Rock Boys Club" after she set two individual records at the state AAU indoor meet. At fourteen-years old, she was a finalist and the only female candidate for the Neil Martin Victory Trophy.

In 1947, at the first Arkansas High School State Championships, Keith was the sole representative of her all-girls Catholic school, Mount St. Mary's. She won two events with state records. The following year, she was a founding member of the swim team at Little Rock Junior College (today, the University of Arkansas at Little Rock).

Some twenty years later, Wrape's former Boys Club teammate Jimmy Miller had become a full-time coach who frequently wrote sports articles for the *Arkansas Gazette*. One article, titled "Mom, Pop Could Swim, Too" mentioned that a second generation of swimmers had begun appearing in Arkansas.

> *"Last week, Mrs. Sue (Keith) Wrape inquired about starting her four boys in the LRBC team. Sue swam under coach Bess Butler, who was a leading water safety instructor in the 1940s and a pioneer in competitive swimming. She had Sue doing 2-3 mile workouts in an era when a half mile was considered a long, hard session. She was one of the finest competitive swimmers in the South—completely dominated the state AAU women's division when there was only one class for women and two divisions for men, those over or under 15 years."*

Wrape, an Arkansas Swimming Hall of Fame inductee, became a nurse and taught swimming to many handicapped children at Little Rock's Camp Aldersgate, as well as to her own six children. Today, she still answers to the name "Splash," a term of endearment given her by many swim students.

Roy Gentry and Bob Shell

Two talented Little Rock swimmers, Roy Gentry and Bob Shell, did not achieve the extended publicity of their peers. Their stories reveal how swimming opportunities, more often than not, are compromised by the demands of the world.

Roy Gentry joined the Air Force when the Korean War started in the summer of 1950. He retired as a colonel in 1978. Back in 1947 and 1948, Gentry was winning swimming races for the Little Rock Boys Club and the new team at Little Rock Junior College. With Gentry as a leading scorer, the Junior College defeated college teams from schools at Conway and Arkadelphia.

Bob Shell was in the fast lane, too. He was seventeen-years old in 1947 and swimming for the YMCA when he beat Tony Koonce and Mickey Gunn in a 200-meter freestyle at the AAU meet at Fair Park Pool. In 1948, Shell swam on a 150-yard medley relay that set a state AAU record. He has kept the original Arkansas AAU certificates for those achievements for more than 60 years.

But despite Shell's initial success, competitive swimming was not the right fit. "I didn't like swimming that much," Shell said. "I went to work after that."

Roy Gentry *demonstrates a proper dive start. Jennings Lake, 1948.*

Today, he directs Baldwin & Shell Construction, one of Arkansas' largest and most successful engineering firms.

By the end of the decade, Arkansas swimming had established itself as a sport with keen public interest and impressive local achievement. Home grown talent had emerged, and local young men and women were recognized as champion athletes. It was an auspicious beginning.

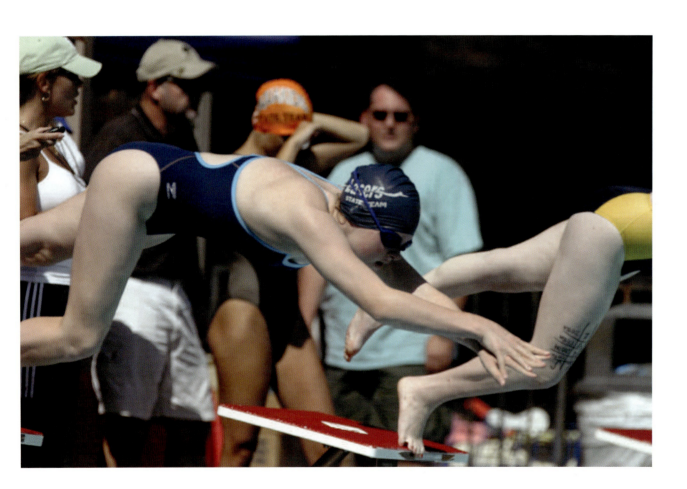

Chapter 2. 1950s

A New Social Phenomenon—The Age Group Swim Meet
Arkansas swimming in the 1950s produced a remarkable number of nationally ranked age-group swimmers. Most of them were in the 10 & Under division. Team rosters grew and clubs hired more coaches. Little Rock's three downtown 20-yard pools were popular, busy places.

The decade opened with Bob Branch winning the Neil Martin Victory Trophy as Arkansas' outstanding amateur athlete. Branch, an honor student at the University of Illinois in 1950, had been a Boys Club swimmer, a state record holder in the 50 meter freestyle (28.0), and a wrestler with state light heavyweight titles in 1947 and 1948. Branch's award was the fourth time since 1946 that a swimmer or diver had been a finalist or winner.

The recognition of aquatics continued through the 1950s. Little Rock newspaper articles and photographs provided frequent reports of swimming meets. A new social phenomenon emerged—the age group swim meet.

In the 1950s, there were no black competitive swimmers in Arkansas. Laws at the time required all public facilities to be segregated. Little Rock would achieve international notoriety in 1957 with the desegregation crisis at Central High School. But well before that civil rights landmark event, the city demonstrated an early separate-but-equal gesture by opening an outdoor pool for African Americans.

The Negro Pool, as the newspaper called it, opened in August 1950 in Gillam Park in southwest Little Rock. An indoor pool opened in 1953 at the new South End Boys Club (later renamed Thrasher Boys Club) at 33rd and Gaines Street. The club was established for "Negro Boys." Some thirty years later, Arkansas' first African American national age group swimming champion, Matt Twillie, would get his start at the Thrasher indoor pool.

Swimming News from Fort Smith, AR

Off to a Flying Start *in the AAU meet at the Boys Club pool Friday night, four of the contestants give fans an idea of the action in the featured races. Little Rock teams copped first and second places in the opening night's action as Johnny Barton made the outstanding individual performance.*
Photo and Caption: *Southwest Times Record,* March 29, 1952

Little Rock Swimmers Dominate AAU Tourney
Little Rock swimmers dominated the Arkansas AAU swim and dive meet here by sweeping all four divisions in the finals at the Boys Club pool Saturday night…. Two first places by Mary Lou Womack gave the Little Rock YWCA the edge over the Little Rock Boys Club, 50-44, for the girls' team crown Saturday night…. The Little Rock Boys Club won midget team, junior boys', and men's divisions.
Southwest Times Record, *March 29, 1953*

> The recognition of aquatics continued through the 1950s. Little Rock newspaper articles and photographs provided frequent reports of swimming meets.

Medley Relay, War Memorial Pool, 1952
The photo captures the crowd and the excitement of the race as breaststrokers are crossing the pool on the second leg of the relay. Look for the butterfly swimmers standing on the blocks in each lane, each boy waiting for his racing start.

Age Group Success

"Midget" swimmers, competitors in the 10 & Under age group, were the darlings of the decade. Other age groups were Junior Boys (11-16), Men (17 and up), and a single category for girls of all ages. New age group categories for 7-8 year olds and 6 & Under swimmers were later added to accommodate the rising number of younger children entering the sport.

This new generation had been recruited from learn-to-swim programs or attracted by newspaper articles that described local and state meets. Little Rock had two daily newspapers, the *Arkansas Gazette* and the *Arkansas Democrat*. This often resulted in double coverage of the victories racked up by the Little Rock Boys Club and the YWCA.

> *"The Little Rock Boys Club swimming team, foremost in Arkansas swimming circles for many years now, displayed its 1951 talent in its home pool last night by sweeping all three divisions in the state AAU indoor swimming and diving championships."*
> — Arkansas Gazette, *April 8, 1951*

The Little Rock teams also swam against military squads from the Millington Naval Base at Memphis. They traveled to meets in Oklahoma, Tennessee, and Indiana. They raced college teams at the University of Kansas, Hendrix College, and state colleges at Conway and Arkadelphia. And they traveled on a summer circuit to state competitions at Fort Smith, Jonesboro, Wilson, and Warren.

The Diving Kingpin

Benny Wise had been swimming at Fair Park Pool and the Boys Club all his youth. He was 14 years old in 1950 when local diver Hardie Thomas became his mentor at War Memorial Pool. Wise, called the "diving kingpin" and one of the most consistent winners of all Arkansas divers, remembered the limiting conditions of the time.

"The board was a stiff solid plank with coca matting," Wise said. "Indoor diving was done at the Boys Club, but with that low ceiling, you had to be careful."

Following other top Arkansas swimmers and divers, Wise attended Northwestern Louisiana State College and competed for the school for three years. A job offer brought him to the professional diving circuit, which included performances at the Atlantic City Steel Pier and other

> **Are Swimmers Smarter Than Other Athletes?**
> "Swimming helps build character more than intelligence. That's the result of a strong work ethic. If you want to be good, you show up."
> — **Sammy Turner**

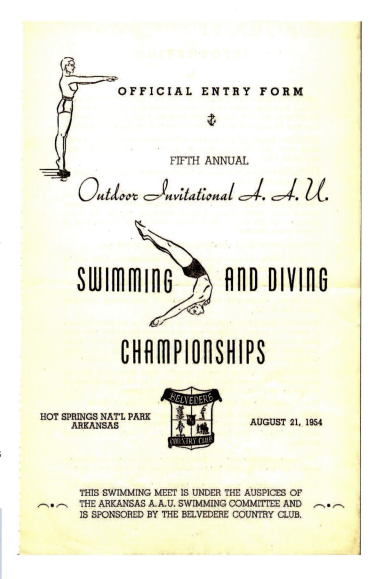

> "A diver is a fair swimmer with his brains knocked loose."
>
> Benny Wise

resorts in the U.S. and Mexico. Professional diving, Wise said, was a seasonal vocation for young, single guys.

In 2010, Wise reflected on the daredevil nature of those, like himself, who leapt from platforms thirty feet and higher.

"A diver is a fair swimmer with his brains knocked loose," Wise explained.

A New Coach at the YWCA

The Little Rock YWCA swim team gained attention in the mid-1950s when local swimmer Mary Lou Jaworski began coaching there. The tall, athletic Jaworski would become a major figure in Arkansas swimming over the next thirty years.

Little Rock had other women swim coaches in this groundbreaking role, including two women associated with the Little Rock Boys Club—Bess Butler in the 1940s and Edith Frazier in the 1950s and 1960s.

The YWCA pool, like those nearby at the Boys Club and YMCA, was not designed for racing. High walls with little gutter spill-over and shallow water depth created extremely choppy conditions. Lane lines, used only for races, were simple nylon ropes with small, widely-spaced plastic floats that guaranteed a water-park wave-pool experience.

Frank Letzig, a swim parent who became a top swimming official in his time, worked many meets amid the crowds, heat, and noise at the YWCA. Letzig said the building maintenance staff was not interested in improving race conditions by adding water and raising the pool surface to the lip of the gutters. Maintaining proper chemical balance in the water was also challenging in an era when swim goggles and chlorine-removing shampoos were unknown concepts. Young swimmers emerging from the Little Rock basement pools were easily distinguished by their bleached hair and their red-rimmed eyes.

In April 1958, Jaworski was honored at a North Little Rock event. The young woman had just completed a season as coach of the new YWCA swim team. Also that season, Jaworski swam on the girls' 160-yard freestyle relay, filling a gap when needed on her team roster.

That year, Jaworski had established the YWCA team as independent of its parent organization, the Little Rock YMCA. She also had the task of managing an 18-month old daughter.

Jaworski started racing as a fourteen-year old for the North Little Rock Boys Club. In the mid 1950s, Jaworski was the top female swimmer in Arkansas, setting

Mary Lou Jaworski, YWCA coach with 8 & Under girls, members of the Peewee Division Championship Team. The swimmers are: (from left) Debbie Landsman, Connie Goss, Betty Robinson, and Barbie Berger.
Photo: North Little Rock Times, 1959

state AAU records in backstroke, individual medley, and freestyle events. In 1953, the future Arkansas Swimming Hall of Fame member went 35.3 in the 50-meter freestyle and 15.5 for the 25-meter free.

YWCA swimmer Autumn Buddenberg Taylor spoke of Jaworski as a friend and teacher. Taylor recalled the July 1969 evening when the team was returning from an out of town swim meet. Jaworski had the bus driver repeatedly pull into hotels along the highway so the girls could be updated on the Neil Armstrong moon landing.

Jan Diner Hildebrandt remembered Jaworski as a coach whose determined assistance helped her become the first young YWCA swimmer to break one minute for the 100-yard freestyle. Hildebrandt said Jaworski was "a great fan and a teacher who took care of us, who was always encouraging her girls."

Even the girl swimmers at the Boys Club knew of the atmosphere created by Jaworski and her assistant coach Mickey Burris. Marc Ann Perrine, a Boys Club swimmer coached by Edith Frazier, said the competing teams were "great rivals and seesawed back and forth on who was winning the most relays." Perrine said she was loyal to Frazier, but the YWCA was probably a more fun girls team.

When Jaworski was promoted to YWCA Executive Director in 1970, she had been successful in modernizing Arkansas AAU rules to allow new age divisions for girls and separation of boys and girls team scores. She had been a swimming teacher to hundreds of children, including two who became Arkansas' first international champions: Keena Rothhammer, Olympic gold medalist in 1972, and Pat Miles, winner at the 1971 Pan American games. And Jaworski would be instrumental in starting the Arkansas Masters Swim program in the 1980s.

But it was back in 1958 that Jaworski stated her personal goals for coaching and age group swimming. "My first thrill is to see one of my girls win, and the second is to see a girl who has lost a race show good sportsmanship."

Recruiting for the Boys Club

Wesley Clark was one of many Little Rock kids who showed up at the Boys Club. The future four-star general and 2004 presidential candidate was attending Pulaski Heights Junior High School in 1957 when Miller posted a bulletin at the school asking boys to try out for his team. In an early demonstration of leadership, Clark rounded up other junior high swimmers and provided a complete new relay team for the Boys Club roster.

Leadership comes early for swimmer Wes Clark

"Five boys from Pulaski Heights walked in to the club, and one of them a real scrawny youngster, said, "I am the captain of the school swim team, and we want to try out." That meeting proved to be the start of quite a swimming career and an enriching experience both for him and me."

By Jimmy Miller, Arkansas Gazette, March 16, 1964

Coached by Miller and L. B. Parker, the Boys Club established a twelve-year winning streak for the state AAU swim title, finally broken in 1958 by a team from Crossett, Arkansas. In 1959, Miller left the Boys Club to begin teaching at a Little Rock junior high school. He had been associated with the Boys Club for more than fifteen years as a swimmer and Assistant Executive Director.

Miller would continue off and on at the Boys Club until he established his own program, the Miller Swim Gym, in the 1960s. But the early 1950s swim teams were those Miller called his best. Top athletes included swimmer Gordon Vineyard, third in nation at the 1951 Junior Olympics and a member of a 1953 relay that had the second fastest time in the nation, and diver Benny Wise, second nationally at a 1952 Junior Olympic meet. Miller is credited with starting the Arkansas Junior Olympic program (from 1953-1956, twenty eight Arkansas swimmers won national championships at Junior Olympics meets) and the state Junior High School swim league.

Miller proudly stated that most of his swimmers receive college scholarships.

Developing swim champions at LRBC is Jimmy Miller's Knack

"If a boy stays with me through high school, I'll get him into college. And I've never had a boy yet that didn't want to go."

Arkansas Democrat, February 9, 1958

Inevitable Departure

Miller's departure from the Boys Club was inevitable. The organization could not support his dreams of bringing swimming to new heights. For Executive Director Billy Mitchell, the Boys Club goal was to serve as many youth as possible, not develop an elite program that only reached a small group.

> "My first thrill is to see one of my girls win, and the second is to see a girl who has lost a race show good sportsmanship."
>
> Mary Lou Jaworski

> "If you were misbehaving in practice, he would pull you out of the pool, make you bend over, put your hands on your knees, take his towel and give you a 'souvenir.'"
>
> Harvey Humphries

Jimmy Miller *and his 10 & Under Little Rock Boys Club team at Memphis, Back: Doug Donoho, Robert Plemmons, Robert Williamson, Rod Carmichael; Middle: Sammy Turner, Clyde Brooks, Ritchie Carmichael, Ryan Collins; Kneeling: Sha Williamson, Frank Plemmons, Kevin Dolan, Ricky Fleenor.* **March 7, 1959**

Miller was also teaching swimming and drown-proofing of toddlers. Some of his early classes were in the pool of the Coachman's Inn, a Little Rock motel. He also taught swimming at the small pool he built at his house on Cleveland Street. Miller even had a greenhouse-style enclosure over the pool for winter training.

The earliest team workouts for the Miller Swim Gym were held in the backyard pool. It required eight lengths for 100 yards, no bottom lines identified lanes, and old nylon ropes were used for lane dividers. Swimmers changed clothes in the house, and came back into the living room after practice, often dripping wet.

Miller was successful in teaching children and babies to swim, but his technique of tossing children into the deep water or dropping them off the diving board alarmed some parents.

A Surrogate Father in a Male Dominated World

A distinct role model in a time before gender equity, Miller was, as swimmer Phil McMath said, a surrogate father in a male dominated world.

If a swimmer didn't take a workout seriously enough, Miller might leap onto him from the pool deck and drag him to the bottom in a leg lock. Or he might bring him up onto the deck and pop him with a towel on his butt.

"If you were misbehaving in practice, he would pull you out of the pool, make you bend over, put your hands on your knees, take his towel and give you a 'souvenir,'" Harvey Humphries said. "No one wanted to cry, but you would see the tears well up. You had to say it didn't hurt."

Miller's physical interactions with his boys would not be tolerated in modern coaching. But in the era when those actions were accepted, they often achieved positive results.

Many of Miller's swimmers started as seven-year olds and stayed with him until they went to college. Those years allowed Miller numerous opportunities to provide the life lessons that fathers usually taught their sons.

A Tough, Inspirational Coach

Miller was a tough, inspirational coach to hundreds of boys in the post-war era. He built team unity by having the entire group repeat a set until every boy achieved the required time. He challenged individuals by holding daily time trials until the swimmer achieved his target.

Wesley Clark called him "a roughneck, not an Ivy Leaguer, an Arkansas guy who had a mystique about him." Miller rode motorcycles. He did clown dives on Sunday with his buddies at War Memorial pool. He had the most shrill, two-fingered whistle anyone had ever heard. Addicted to cigarettes and black coffee, Miller risked being fired from the Boys Club by standing in the shower room door and smoking during team practice. The kids would warn him if Mitchell was coming.

Some sessions at the Boys Club, Miller would sit in the shallow end of the pool, stopping his young swimmers at the turn to put them on his knee and show them, holding their hands, how the stroke should go.

"Jimmy radiated this strong care about your child. He could do things with them and then hug them. They would do anything for him," Sara Kay Humphries, mother of Harvey Humphries and a Miller age group swimmer herself, said. "Each swimmer thought, 'I'm the special one.' Jimmy had that gift."

Miller arranged for his older Boys Club swimmers to work as counselors at the Pfeifer Kiwanis Camp, where he held daily workouts at the 25-meter pool. But Miller also put his camp counselors through challenging and hilarious tests. Wesley Clark recalls episodes when Miller made his teenaged swimmers eat live minnows or jump into the Little Maumelle River from the upper girders of the infamous Red Bridge.

"The stuff that would drive you crazy about him was what made you love him," Harvey Humphries said. "He was always teaching you something when he was coaching."

Miller's swimmers also spoke of the "sugar shack," a rough camp site located on a few wooded acres west of Little Rock. Miller's property had a creek flowing through it. The water was deep enough to serve as a rustic 50-meter training site, complete with milk jug floats holding rope lane lines. Humphries remembered the site where young swimmers slept in tents on the ground.

"One day Miller saw a snake in the creek. He pulled it out and beat it with a stick on the mud bank until it was dead. Then, he said to us, 'Okay, you're ready to swim now,'" Humphries said. "The girls were screaming and crying. You couldn't believe what you were going through there, but you didn't want to miss it."

An Immense Love for Children

But it was Miller's immense love for children that is most remembered. "I have never known anyone as dedicated to helping kids as Jimmy Miller," Mickey Gunn said.

"Jimmy's philosophy," his widow Boonie Miller said, "was that all children on the team would swim. A team is not just the champions. Behind the champions are those who pushed them every day to go fast. So, all kids got to swim on the relays. No matter how fast you were, you never just sat on the bench."

Miller was a big brother who told hair-raising ghost stories at campfires. He was a father figure who guided boys though emotional phases of growth. And he was a demanding coach who used both respect and corporal punishment to bring out the best in his swimmers.

> "Jimmy radiated this strong care about your child. He could do things with them and then hug them. They would do anything for him. Each swimmer thought, 'I'm the special one.' Jimmy had that gift."
>
> Sara Kay Humphries

Great Night for a Water Meet

A hard downpour scarcely bothered anyone at the state schoolboy swimming meet at War Memorial Park's pool last night—at least not these two competitors. Charles Matthews, right, a North Sider representing Catholic High, set a flock of records, and Jeff Wilson, left, was a point maker for Little Rock High.
Photo and caption: Arkansas Gazette, August 6, 1953

"Jimmy could give you a look of disapproval that was almost as bad as being popped with a towel," Mike Stewart, a Boys Club swimmer in the 1950s, said. "But his best features were his smile and laugh. They were contagious."

Stewart said he was small for his age and frustrated from competing against bigger and stronger boys. Miller sensed the problem and had several talks with Stewart at the Pfeifer Camp after other campers were in bed. Stewart said Miller told him they would work on distance races, stamina, and techniques to compensate for the size disadvantage.

"He told me when you were at a disadvantage, you had to work harder and smarter to overcome your opponent," Stewart said. "I used these principles later in college and in my career in commercial sales."

Mike Barden, a Boys Club sprinter from the 1960s, also learned professional skills from Miller. Barden, who worked as a swim coach for nearly thirty years, said Miller instilled in him self-confidence and a sense of self-worth through swimming.

"On our team trips in Miller's station wagon, he always had me in the front with the heat sheets, talking to him. He saw something in me I didn't know I had. It wasn't until many years later when I realized how privileged I was to be there with him," Barden said.

> **What is the difference between sprinters and distance swimmers?**
> "As a sprinter, I still have to count in fours."
> **Mike Barden**

Chapter 3. 1960s

National Age Group Rankings, Better Pools And Coaching
An era of growth and expansion, the 1960s saw new Little Rock families enroll their children in local swimming programs. Numerous central Arkansas age group swimmers attained #1 national rankings and set national records in 20-yard pools. Competitive swimming shifted to a more dedicated and demanding club environment.

Why Choose the Y

With nearly identical swimming facilities at the YMCA and the Boys Club, choosing a membership was not a difficult decision for most Little Rock youngsters.

Membership at the YMCA was about $10 per year in 1960. At the Boys Club, it was virtually free. The Little Rock YMCA had a dormitory and a range of services for adults. In comparison, the Boys Club was a kid's paradise, a place to hang out all day playing basketball, wrestling, and shooting pool. The Boys Club sponsored the extremely popular "Knot Hole Gang," which provided free entry for children to Arkansas Travelers minor league baseball games.

At the Boys Club, younger boys swam naked during free swim time, a policy to maintain pool cleanliness. The nude swimming policy caused some hilarious moments. Friday afternoon was parent visiting day, and the bleachers were often filled with swim team families. The pool area echoed with screams and laughter whenever a naked boy, forgetting the weekly schedule, came rushing to the pool.

But the difference between the Boys Club and the YMCA/YWCA was more than bathing suits. YMCA families generally had a higher social standing than Boys Club families. That distinction became a key element in the late 1960s when the newly established Little Rock Racquet Club began attracting swimmers away from the three established downtown teams.

"The YMCA was the club of privilege," Tom Roberts, a YMCA swimmer, said. "At the Y, we were all prima donnas. We wore suits, but at the Boys Club, they all swam naked. And they still kicked our butts."

Swimming Thrives in Arkansas, Interest in swimming on an upswing in Arkansas.
".... more than 400 participants at a state AAU meet in Monticello, Arkansas, surpassing the previous high attendance of 175 participants. Coach Edith Frazier, with 68 swimmers on her Boys Club girls' team, said she had only eight swimmers four years earlier, but 'now we have to turn girls away all the time.'"
Arkansas Democrat, June 6, 1961

Nationally Ranked Age Group Swimmers

Through the 1960s, Central Arkansas swimmers set many National Age Group records in the 20-yard pool category. A remarkable number of them were ranked as #1 in the nation in their events. Many others were listed in the National Top 5 for the age groups.

This profusion of nationally ranked swimmers reflected a growing participation in a fairly new activity. National records were rapidly being established and surpassed. Also, the Arkansas swimmers were racing in 20-yard pools, which were the common size for Boys Clubs and YMCAs across the nation. A larger number of swimmers nationally were racing in 25-

> "The YMCA was the club of privilege. At the Y, we were all prima donnas. We wore suits, but at the Boys Club, they all swam naked. And they still kicked our butts."
>
> Tom Roberts

"I never dreamed of winning. Our kids were better than we thought. Now they know they are getting good."

Edith Frazier

Team Portraits, 1961
At the Little Rock YMCA, a team photo shoot was a dress-up event. At the Boys Club, a team bathing suit was adequate for the swimmers and coach.

(Right) Little Rock YMCA team, Coach Miles Donoho.

(Below) Little Rock Boys Club, Coach Jimmy Miller.

yard and 50-meter pools. Separate national records were kept for each of the categories.

Nevertheless, Central Arkansas' age group swimmers in the 1960s were the best for their time and place. Some of these achievements included:

National Age Group Records, 10 & Under

1960   160-Yard Medley Relay (1:52.7) – LRBC: Sammy Turner, Doug Donoho, Ricky Fleenor, Clyde Brooks.

1960   200-Meter (LC) Medley Relay (2:50.1) – LRBC: Kevin Dolan, Doug Donoho, Ricky Fleenor, Clyde Brooks.

1965   100-Yard Butterfly (1:13.6) – LRBC: Marc Ann Bryan. Bryan is Top 5 in five events that year.

1966   200-Yard Freestyle (2:16.4) and 100-Yard Freestyle (1:02.7). YMCA: Greg Martin.

1966   40-Yard Freestyle (23.6) and 80-Yard Individual medley (1:02.6). YMCA: Kathy Sullivan

(Continued on page 44)

Are Swimmers Smarter Than Other Athletes?
"Sprinters are smarter than distance swimmers because we get finished faster and can party sooner."
Mary Lou Jaworski

No Shortage of Talent

Nearly fifty girls posed with coach Edith Frazier for this 1961 swim team photo at the Little Rock Boys Club. The team roster increased to sixty girls just a few years later.

A large number of swimmers gave the Boys Club an advantage in most meets, but Frazier's girls had talent as well. In March 1959, they won the team championship at the Open Age Group and AAU meet at the Memphis Navy Air Station in Millington.

"I never dreamed of winning," Frazier told the Arkansas Gazette. "Our kids were better than we thought. Now they know they are getting good."

Frazier's four children swam for the Boys Club. Daughter Edith Lynn is in the 4th row, kneeling, 2nd from right. Youngest daughter Linda is in the front row, second from right.

"In this photo, I'm wearing my first suit that Mom made me from scraps of other suits," Linda Frazier Bland said in 2010. "I was so small no bathing suit fit me. I was four years old, and my first race was at Hendrix College that year."

Donna de Verona conducted a swimming clinic at War Memorial Pool in Little Rock in August 1961. The 13-year old had won two gold medals and was the youngest swimmer at the 1960 Olympics. A Boys Club relay team receives a trophy and looks on in awe:
(top left) Ricky Fleanor, (top right) Sha Williamson, (lower left) Clyde Brooks, (lower right) Sammy Turner.

New national age group record
*10 & Under, 200-Meter Medley Relay
2:50.1, July 23, 1960.*

Little Rock Boys Club team: Kevin Dolan (top left), Clyde Brooks (top right), Ricky Fleenor (lower left), and Doug Donoho (lower right).

Sammy Turner *is in the center photo on the cover of Junior Swimmer magazine, February 1961. The magazine was the primary information source for swimming and national age group records at the time.*

The Little Rock Boys Club 10 & Under medley relay team is shown below Turner's photo. From left: Ricky Fleenor, Sammy Turner, George West, Clyde Brooks. This team had the fastest time in the country for the 200-Yard Medley Relay and was Top 5 in three other relay events. Clyde Brooks was Top 5 in three solo events.

New national age group record
10 & Under, 160-Yard Medley Relay, 1:52.7, February 27, 1960

Little Rock Boys Club team (top to bottom): Doug Donoho, backstroke; Clyde Brooks, butterfly; Sammy Turner, freestyle; and Ricky Fleenor, breaststroke.

Memphis VALENTINE meet
February 10-11, 1968
We were especially proud of Kathy in this meet, and she certainly deserved to do well. The girls won the 10 & Under division and for the first time we have some good qualifiers in the 11-12 with Kathy Letzig and Diane Letzig.

A Valentine With Ribbons

Kathy Sullivan, 12-year old swimmer for the Little Rock YWCA team, turned in her best times of her four-year career over the weekend at Memphis. She swam the 100-Yard Backstroke in 1:12 to win and posted a 1:02.8, good for second in the 100-Yard Freestyle.
Arkansas Gazette, February 12, 1968

In her own words… Pages from Mary Lou Jaworski's scrapbooks

Memphis, April 27-28, 1963
…presented us with the Sweepstakes trophy after the girls had tossed Mickey and me in fully dressed. Never have we had a happier moment than this.

RELAY TEAM WINNERS
… Susan Brooks, Jan Diner, Lisa Adams, Patty Bowen

This YWCA 8 & Under team won the 100-Yard Medley Relay and set a meet record at the Cotton Capitol Invitational Swim Meet at the Memphis Athletic Club. Four hundred swimmers from six states competed. **The YWCA team swam it in 1:20.0, taking 17 seconds off the record.**
December 24, 1966

Warren, Junior Olympics
June 22-23, 1968
We won the total sweepstakes! What a nice way to start out the summer season. We took all four of the girls divisions, too. The girls really outdid themselves.

YWCA'S Record-breakers

Members of the Little Rock YWCA team who broke records in the Arkansas Junior Olympic Short Course Swimming Championships at Warren. In front, Diane Letzig, 200-Yard Freestyle and 200-Yard Individual Medley; from left, Kathy Sullivan, 200-Yard Freestyle and 100-Yard Backstroke; Susan Brooks, 200-Yard Individual Medley; and Margaret Bost, 50-Yard Freestyle.
Arkansas Gazette, June 24, 1968

Little Rock YMCA 8 and Under swimmers won their division and set four pool records at the Shreveport East Ridge Country Club. The YMCA boys swam the 100-Yard Medley Relay in 1:15.7 and the 100-Yard Freestyle Relay in 1:05.5. Relay swimmers are (top to bottom) Edward Lile, Jay Kincannon, Ricky Witherspoon, and Jim Handloser.
Little Rock YWCA girls won their division and broke three pool marks.
Photo and caption: Arkansas Gazette, July 4, 1967

Little Rock YMCA, YWCA Teams Capture Shreveport 8-under Titles

YMCA's Record-Breakers

Are Swimmers Smarter than Other Athletes?

"Swimmers are in a sensory deprivation tank when doing their work. And they have to work year round. They have less free time, so they are more creative and more disciplined than other athletes, so their academics can be better. Most of their successes are private, not public. They do it to better themselves."

Harvey Humphries

#1 National Age Group Ranking, 10 & Under

1960   80-Yard Medley Relay, (no time available) – LRBC: Gail Allen, Debbie Gassaway, Ann Benkovitz, Edith Frazier.

1961   200-Yard Medley Relay. (no time available) – LRBC: George West, Mark Stockton, Sammy Turner, Ricky Fleenor, and Clyde Brooks. The Boys Club relay team was in the National Top 5 in four events, and Clyde Brooks was listed as Top 5 for three solo events.

Also in 1961, Boys Club swimmer Frank Pirnique won the Junior National Championships at Bartlesville, OK in 1:01.6 in the 100-Yard Backstroke, just .6 seconds off the national record.

In 1963, five relay teams and two individual Boys Club swimmers, Richard Turner and Jan Marak, were in the National Top 5.

In 1964, the YMCA 10 & Under relay team of Chip Gatchell, Pat Miles, Doug Martin, and Walter Stevens had Top 5 times for the 160-Yard Medley Relay (1:55.7) and Freestyle Relay (1:40.9).

In 1967, Pat Miles began to gain attention, setting 13-14 National Age Group records in the 500-Yard Freestyle (5:02.7) and 200-Yard Backstroke (2:09.9).

The achievements of Arkansas age group swimmers culminated in 1969, with more than forty of them listed as Top 5 in the nation. (See Appendix B)

Growth and Popularity

Participation at state swim meets increased rapidly. In 1965, more than 600 swimmers raced at the Hendrix AAU Invitational at Conway, making it the largest meet in Arkansas swim history. Forty-five new state records were set, and the Little Rock Boys Club was the overall winner.

The growth and popularity of swimming in Little Rock was most influenced by Jimmy Miller. He was teaching swimming to more than 1,100 kids annually. His Boys Club team had 150 swimmers in six age groups, and many college scholarships had been awarded. Miller was also writing articles for the *Arkansas Gazette*. From 1964 to 1967 alone, Miller had more than twenty feature-length swimming stories published in the newspaper.

Some Arkansas swimmers attain national attention
by Jimmy Miller
"A competitive swimmer in Arkansas is a boy or girl who from age 4 to 30 is willing to give up all recognition of school sports, be a minority group member, be laughed at for swimming in the winter and still stay with his sport in spite of the opposition, poor facilities, poor budgets, poor public support, and lack of swimming in the high schools."
Arkansas Gazette, January 16, 1964

Miller wrote about the value of the sport for swimmers and families. He profiled top age group athletes of the time, his own Boys Club champions, as well as other team standouts, such as Judy Smith and Diane Letzig of the YWCA. Miller praised the officials who worked the swim meets, and he lauded parents for their support:

"Family support…is not something that comes easy. It takes a dedicated parent to go through car pools, specials diets, wet hair, runny noses, re-arranged mealtimes, and pre-arranged vacations in order to meet schedules."

Miller's articles often reminded readers of swimming's long-term benefit.

"All of this troublesome and time consuming work pays off for parents who are willing to meet the challenge. The most rewarding prize is not the medal or the public recognition, but the assurance that their child is leading a good life and will usually make an honest effort to continue his swimming in college."

Miller even wrote about other Little Rock coaches, such as John Hays at the YMCA, praising him for a learn-to-swim program that introduced children as young as four years old to the sport.

Keena Rothhammer, *8 years old in 1965, swam for the Little Rock YWCA. She would win gold and bronze medals at the 1972 Olympics.*

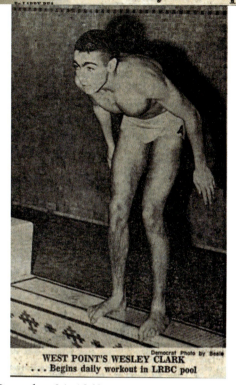

December 24, 1963
Home for the holidays from West Point, Wesley Clark worked out at the Little Rock Boys Club. The future four-star general and presidential candidate was ranked #1 in his class and was competing on the Army swim team.

Groundbreaking at the Miller Swim Gym, January 1968
Jimmy and Boonie Miller begin construction of Little Rock's first 50-meter pool.

The cigarette foil trophy cup was created by Miller from the packs of cigarettes he constantly smoked. It was given to swimmers who had a good workout. The Miller Swim Gym patch was another team keepsake.

Changing the Balance of Power

In a 1963 AAU meet at Fort Smith, state records were broken in 48 of the 66 events. The high rate of record-setting swims continued through the 1960s. The surge in swimming's popularity strengthened the teams at the Little Rock YMCA and YWCA. The balance of power shifted in 1965 when the YMCA team for the first time defeated the Boys Club at the state championship meet.

"Historically, the Boys' Club had always won because Miller would call out the hordes for the state meet. At that meet, we finally had enough depth to beat them even though they still had at least twice as many swimmers. That always felt like a turning point to me, because that was when quality and training started to beat quantity."
Doug Martin

At this time, the YWCA team had an unbeatable 8-year old named Keena Rothhhammer. The Rothhammers moved to Texas and then California, where Keena trained with top swim coaches. The journey culminated at the 1972 Olympics, where Keena won a gold medal in the 800-Meter Freestyle and a bronze in the 200-Meter Freestyle.

As the YMCA and YWCA teams grew and improved, Miller was also in transition. In addition to teaching in a

Little Rock public school, he was teaching swimming part time, coaching the Boys Club age group swim team, and writing articles for the *Arkansas Gazette*. He and wife Boonie were also raising nine children.

Miller was also planning the next stage of Arkansas swimming, the construction of better pools. His newspaper articles drew attention to the limited facilities in Little Rock and the restriction that was placing on the sport.

Some Arkansas Swimmers Attain National Attention
by Jimmy Miller
"Until some effort is made to expand the interest of swimming in Arkansas and develop new facilities with properly trained coaches, we will continue to lose our finest young participants in this sport to out-of-state colleges and out-of-state jobs."
Arkansas Gazette, January 16, 1964

Miller left the Boys Club a final time in the mid 1960s. The Miller Swim Gym team included many swimmers who left the Boys Club to follow their coach. Workouts were held in Miller's tiny backyard pool and other sites around Little Rock where the team could squeeze in.

Little Rock's first 50-meter pool

By 1970, Miller Swim Gym had built Little Rock's first 50-meter competitive pool. This was a remarkable achievement, but it introduced distinct financial management and planning responsibilities. Miller was an enthusiastic and dedicated coach, but he was less experienced in the business of maintaining a team and operating a large outdoor pool. Several of his swim parents assisted in obtaining construction finances and creating operational plans for the new site.

The Boys Club continued to have a strong swim team for a few years following Miller's departure. The first coach was John Torbett, who was also coaching and teaching full time at the University of Arkansas at Little Rock (UALR), formerly Little Rock Junior College. Torbett recruited two swim parents to help him at the Boys Club. John Brooks took over the age group program, and Jud Bryan coached the senior boys.

Arkansas Democrat, December 19, 1966

This shuffling of coaches and the emergence of new swim teams was a clear sign that change was in the air. The late 1960s also marked the end of the 20-yard pool era in Arkansas. Although many state swimmers were rated in the Top 5 nationally, there was a pressing need for better pools and full-time coaches.

Chapter 3. 1960s

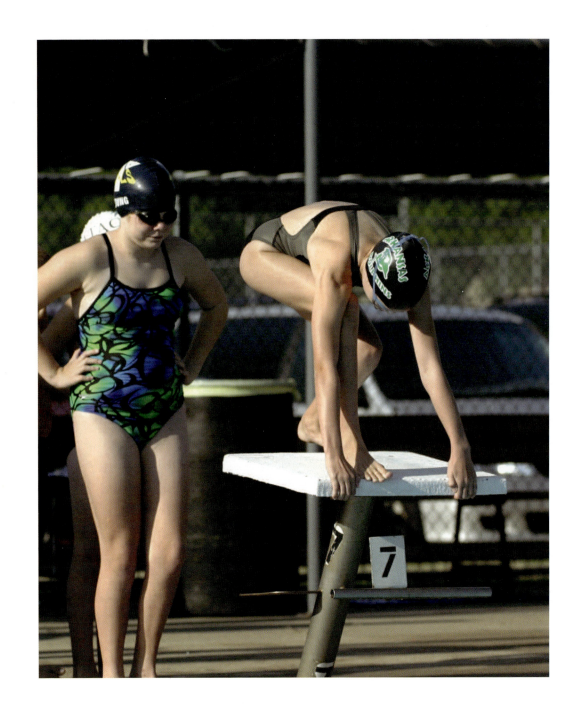

Chapter 4. Little Rock Racquet Club

A Focus on Athletic Excellence
The opening of the Little Rock Racquet Club in 1967 accelerated the evolution of competitive swimming in Arkansas. Included in the Club's Creed was an ambitious objective to develop Olympic swimmers. That vision was made possible by an eight-lane 25-yard pool and national caliber coaches who set high-level goals for their swimmers.

In 1963, two Little Rock swim parents were relaxing after working as swim meet officials in Jonesboro, Arkansas. Ollie Gatchell was an architect with one of the largest firms in the state. Pat Riley, Sr., a graduate of Harvard Business School, was an executive at a tile manufacturing plant. They were discussing the opportunities swimming offered their children and the lack of facilities in Arkansas.

Both men were athletes. Gatchell had been a Southwest Conference track champion while attending the University of Arkansas. Riley was an active adult tennis player with a number of tournament wins. Both men had children swimming for the Little Rock YMCA and YWCA. And both were familiar with the limited facilities that characterized those programs.

"During swim meets at the Y and the Boys Club, the crowds and low ceilings made the noise almost unbearable," Riley said. "And limited pool space allowed our youngsters only three days a week for workouts. The YMCA director told me they had a number of people to appease and that competitive swimming was not part of their creed."

"I tried to change all that and move to another level," Riley said. "The two things needed were a state of the art facility and an atmosphere that encouraged excellence."

Riley and Gatchell proposed an organization focused on the development of competitive swimming and tennis. They saw the two sports as team activities that appealed to children, adults, and families.

Southern Prejudice

Riley was determined that an established southern prejudice excluding Jewish families from local country clubs would not be continued at the new club. When membership meetings began, Riley asked Jewish businessman Sam Strauss, Jr., to become involved.

"I made Sam prominent and asked for his help in recruiting additional Jewish families," Riley said. "We carefully handled that situation, and soon after there were

Early patch of the Little Rock Racquet Club featured swimming and tennis. The "Splash Racquet Club" was the first choice for the new club's name.

"The two things needed were a state of the art facility and an atmosphere that encouraged excellence."

Pat Riley, Sr.

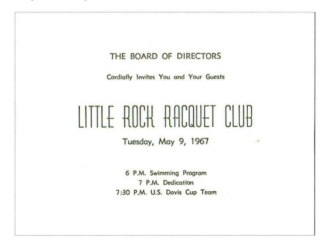

> "It was a matter of faith by all participants, as they could not actually walk onto the land and view the location, which was in a highly undeveloped state. This expression of faith by the membership was symptomatic of the entire endeavor."
>
> Pat Riley, Sr.

Jewish members at the Little Rock Country Club. We broke the barrier."

Seven original board members were elected as club officers. They were Jeff Davis, James Penick, Jr., J. J. Freeman, Robert Rainey, Oliver Gatchell, Pat Riley, and Sam Strauss, Jr. Each signed a demand note for $800, a significant investment at the time. The original membership drive, with active assistance from wives Caroline Gatchell and Martha Riley, eventually brought in 160 families. A presentation at the elite Top of the Rock Club secured another forty memberships in one night.

"It was a matter of faith by all participants, as they could not actually walk onto the land and view the location, which was in a highly undeveloped state," Riley said.

Arkansas Governor Winthrop Rockefeller *at the ribbon cutting ceremony for the Little Rock Racquet Club, May 9, 1967. Club founders Pat Riley, Sr. stands to his right, and Ollie Gatchell is second from the left. Tennis great Arthur Ashe and other members of the 1967 US Davis Cup Team attended the opening ceremony and played a demonstration match.*

"Plans for the facilities were not exact, but were ideas of what could be done. This expression of faith by the membership was symptomatic of the entire endeavor."

Gatchell and Riley began searching for land in Little Rock, visiting tennis and swimming clubs in other cities, and conducting membership meetings. Riley also began promoting the concept of a nonprofit organization owned by its members to other business and community leaders.

Friends in High Places

Riley and other board members worked for leading businesses, and they had friends in high places. Many of the development efforts were contributed by board members and their companies, including notable assistance from architectural firm Ginocchio-Cromwell and Associates.

"They saw the vision I had and liked it. It was a vision they had themselves," Riley said.

Business connections also assisted in obtaining land for the club. A new residential subdivision was being developed in west Little Rock by Dr. and Mrs. Ted Bailey. The Bailey's gave Riley an option for 10.4 acres in the new Foxcroft neighborhood.

Interim financing was provided by First National Bank and Worthen Bank and Trust Company. In July 1965, articles of incorporation were filed. That same year, Witt Stephens, then President and

Chairman of the Board of Arkansas Louisiana Gas Company, committed to a loan. As work on the tennis and swimming facilities got under way, a clubhouse was added to accommodate the increasing memberships. A year later, with construction costs and interest rates rising, Stephens graciously agreed to increase the loan at the original rate.

In 1966, months before the pool was completed, a swim team was established. Youth exercise and weight lifting were directed by swimming instructor Audris "Zeke" Zidermanis. Swimmer Doug Martin, whose family was one of the first to transfer to the new club from the YMCA, recalled the initial strength-building program used iron bars attached to coffee cans filled with concrete. Workouts were conducted in the basement of a commercial building owned by swim parent Lawrence Witherspoon.

A Dedication Program

When the Racquet Club dedication program was conducted on May 9, 1967, the site featured Arkansas' first eight-lane, year-round 25-yard pool and tennis courts. Professional coaches had been hired for the swimming and tennis programs.

Guests at the dedication included Governor Winthrop Rockefeller, Lt. Governor Maurice "Footsie" Britt, and Little Rock Mayor Martin Borchert. A highlight of the evening was an exhibition

AAU swimming meet at the new LRRC pool, August 1968.
Outdoor meets in a well designed 25-yard competitive pool were a welcome change from the crowded conditions of the Little Rock Boys Club and other indoor facilities.

First coaches *for the new LRRC swim team were Edith Frazier, former girls coach at the Little Rock Boys Club, and John Hays, former men's coach at the YMCA.*

"They saw the vision I had and liked it. It was a vision they had themselves."

Pat Riley, Sr.

> "I can remember in the summer or winter just wanting to be up there. Sometimes I'd walk there in the snow just to be at the pool."
>
> Doug Martin

tennis match by four members of the U.S. Davis Cup team, including Arthur Ashe. Attendance by the Davis Cup team was underwritten by the Bailey's.

In his dedication remarks, Riley spoke of the need for championship facilities, professional coaching, and an atmosphere that encouraged excellence. Riley identified the club's plan to prepare swimmers for the 1972 and 1976 Olympics and to groom tennis players for the U.S. Davis Cup team. His lofty goals were incorporated as the Little Rock Racquet Club Creed.

From the Little Rock Racquet Club Creed

We believe that competitive athletics teaches that work, sacrifice, competitive drive, perseverance, selflessness, and respect for authority are the price one must pay to achieve worthwhile goals.

The Club… [will] place first emphasis on providing the ultimate physical facilities for competitive swimming and competitive tennis …. We will staff these facilities with outstanding professional coaches who are excellent instructors.

Where our youth are concerned, we hope to develop Davis Cup tennis players and Olympic swimmers, but more importantly, we hope to develop fine young men and women who will take their place in life as responsible citizens. We will not let our high goals discourage the less athletically inclined, but plan to tailor programs to the needs of all.

We are at a place of beginning in the Little Rock Racquet Club, and we may mold our membership according to these principles. So let us resolve to make this adventure worthy of our best aspirations.

Riley's vision for the club attracted Little Rock's new rising middle class, a group eager for healthy engaging activity for their baby boomer children. It was an idea whose time had come.

"When the Racquet Club came along in 1967, it appealed to some of the more affluent parents that were by then living in the suburbs and didn't want to drive downtown to the YMCA or the Boys Club anymore," Marc Ann Bryan Perrine, a top swimmer for the Little Rock Boys Club girls' team in the 1960s, said. "The Racquet Club opened with great fanfare and a space-age plastic dome over its pool."

A State of Change

Swimming in Little Rock was in a state of change. Boys Club swim coach Jimmy Miller had struck out on his own and established the Miller Swim Gym. The Little Rock YMCA and the YWCA teams would continue for a few more years, but many of their top swimmers joined the Racquet Club.

The YMCA not only lost swimmers, but its last swim coach as well. In 1966, John Hays, who had formal training as an opera singer, left his YMCA job to pursue a performance career. He returned to Little Rock a year later and replaced Zidermanis as the first Racquet Club swim coach.

"It was a good thing when the Racquet Club came in, but the other programs started going downhill," Frank Letzig, a swim parent and prominent swim meet official, said.

The changing dynamics of the local swim scene presented a challenge to the YMCA, the YWCA, and the Boys Club teams. Billy Mitchell, long-time director at the Boys Club and a man widely admired for his dedication to youth, tried to use AAU rules to block the new team.

In 1966, AAU rules required a one-year "unattached" status for swimmers that changed teams. That year, the new LRRC swimmers went to a meet in Shreveport, Louisiana. Although they competed as individuals, a newspaper write up identified them as members of the Little Rock Racquet Club team.

Mitchell scheduled a board meeting of the state AAU. He proposed the Racquet Club team be banned for three years for the rule violation. Riley had his own interpretation of the meeting request. "He didn't want his team to be outscored by ours," Riley said.

Riley recalled the meeting and his response to Mitchell's request for the suspension.

"I challenged Mitchell on the idea that he was punishing the young children and going against the Boys Club mission. He was attacking a group just because they were not under his domain. I told him he should be ashamed of himself. There was silence, and Ollie Gatchell simply said, "One more thought, Mr. Mitchell. We are going to beat you, and we are going to beat you in the pool."

The state AAU board voted in favor of the Racquet Club. By 1967, the team was officially sanctioned for competition.

A Step Up for Arkansas Swimmers

The Racquet Club's eight-lane, 25-yard pool helped Arkansas swimmers discover a new potential in themselves.

"I just wanted to be the fastest I could be," Doug Martin said. "The Racquet Club facilities had more room so you could do more quality workouts. You could host meets and invite teams from out of state. We thought we were in heaven compared to the YMCA."

Martin recalled the Racquet Club as a fun place for kids. In the winter, hot air coming through the blowers kept the bubble-covered pool area warm and comfortable, he said. With the bubble removed in the summer, the pool felt wide open and free.

"I can remember in the summer or winter just wanting to be up there," Martin said. "Sometimes I'd walk there in the snow just to be at the pool."

In the Bubble
The inflatable bubble allowed year-round swimming. Swim team members assisted in bubble installation to prepare for winter swimming. When the club's 50-meter pool was installed in the 1970s, swimmers would scrub the empty pool each spring to ready it for summer training. Coaches tried to make the work day into a team-building activity.

Pool Maintenance Memories
"I did the bubble takedown every year, and I've got a scar to prove it. I remember swimmers would fall into the tarp and disappear. It was like a big waterbed. We'd also scrub the 50-meter pool with Comet and little brushes." **Basil Hicks**

"We dragged the bubble, and I may need hand surgery today as a result. We also used hydrochloride on the pool floor before the summer season, just mopping the pure acid onto the surface of the pool." **Linda Frazier Bland**

"Snow had caked on top of the bubble and collapsed it. One of the poles punctured through. All the ice and snow had gone into the pool. I remember going down to the Racquet Club and clawing out these chunks of ice so we could get the bubble off the water and patch it. It was an all-day ordeal." **Noel Strauss**

> "The other coaches and programs were something to be aware of. The Racquet Club originated from these programs, and the first years we had a very difficult time to be even Arkansas champions. They had national age group champions and record holders. I do not talk about a lone individual. There were relay teams at the national level."
>
> Kees Oudegeest

Within a few years, Riley's vision of Arkansas swimming gaining world recognition became a reality. In 1971, a Racquet Club swimmer, Pat Miles, won a gold medal at the Pan American Games in the 1500 Freestyle. Another, Linda Frazier, was ranked 10th in the world in the mile. Both swimmers had started in the 20-yard pools of the YMCA and Boys Club.

These achievements were clearly built on the strong swimming community in place before the Racquet Club.

"The other coaches and programs were something to be aware of," Kees Oudegeest, LRRC coach from 1969-1973, said. "The Racquet Club originated from these programs, and the first years we had a very difficult time to be even Arkansas champions. They had national age group champions and record holders. I do not talk about a lone individual. There were relay teams at the national level."

Over the next thirty years, the Racquet Club and its newly named "Dolphins Swim Team" gained prestige as a place where an athlete could develop the potential to be a national caliber swimmer under the tutelage of a qualified and successful coach. College athletes returned to Little Rock to swim with the Racquet Club in the summer. College swimmers from schools around the country joined them. Families from outlying Arkansas cities drove to Little Rock so their children could participate. The high quality of Dolphins swimming had a far-reaching impact.

"I will go so far as to say it wasn't just Little Rock, but Arkansas swimming in general," Matt Twillie said. A national age group champion for the Dolphins and a Southwest Conference champion for Southern Methodist University, Twillie was a direct beneficiary of the high expectations and demanding program at the Racquet Club.

"The club played a major role in the 70s, 80s, and 90s because of the talent it produced and the longevity of the Dolphins team success."

> **What is the Difference between Sprinters and Distance Swimmers?**
> "To be a sprinter, you have to be incredibly focused and have those fast twitch muscles. To be a distance swimmer, you have to be kind of crazy and persistent."
>
> **Rick Witherspoon**

1967

Chapter 5. 1970s

New Coaches, New Champions
In the 1970s, local swimmers achieved unprecedented results and fulfilled the Little Rock Racquet Club creed of producing champions. A local boy won a gold medal at the Pan American Games and a teen aged girl earned Top10 world ranking. The decade brought new coaches and shifting team memberships as the caliber of swimming improved.

Jimmy Miller had bragging rights when he wrote, "State Swimming's Little Ripple Grows to Full Splash in Decade." The 1970 article mentioned that four schools—Hendrix College, John Brown University, and the University of Arkansas campuses at Fayetteville and Little Rock—had built new pools. Miller also wrote about a new 50-meter pool in Little Rock, though he declined to identify it belonging to his own Miller Swim Gym.

Swimming in Little Rock continued to change and improve. The Little Rock YMCA dropped its competitive program after many swimming families switched membership to the new Racquet Club. The Boys Club team, as well, would shut down within a few years.

In 1970, Miller's Swim Gym opened its new 50-meter pool in West Little Rock. Three years later, Miller's committed swim parents helped build an indoor 25-yard pool on the site. Never at a loss to seize an opportunity, Miller placed signs along the highway advertising drown-proofing lessons for infants and children.

A summer meet at the Racquet Club in 1972 was attended by 750 swimmers, the largest gathering in Arkansas swimming history, according to meet director Jerry Heil. The failure of the electronic starting system did not deter Ollie Gatchell, who launched many events by holding up his hand in a gun shape and shouting "Boom!" to start the races.

As swimming advanced at the Racquet Club, some tennis-oriented board members disapproved of the program expenses and the swim meet crowds. The tension between swimming and tennis supporters would continue for the next twenty years, contributing to a change of club ownership in the late 1990s.

But in 1973, the Racquet Club increased its investment in swimming, building a 50-meter competitive pool on its grounds.

Credit to the Coaches
"The coach makes the swimmer. The children want to come to the pool for you."
— Mary Oudegeest Brann

"LRRC aims at an Olympic swimmer"
The Little Rock Racquet Club is ready to improve Arkansas' national status and swimming. Step one was to hire Kees and Mary Oudegeest as new swimming coaches. Kees will take on head duties, and Mary will be his assistant. Step number two is to turn them loose.
— Arkansas Democrat, January 25, 1972

The first wave of success at the Racquet Club can be attributed to the Dutch couple, Kees and Mary Oudegeest. The Oudegeests arrived in Little Rock in 1969. Early that year, Kees had brought his East St. Louis YMCA swim team to a meet at Hendrix College. He was recruited and hired by John Bonds, chairman of the LRRC Swimming Committee.

"We want a swimmer in the Olympics. That's why we hired Oudegeest. No other Arkansas coach has had Olympic experience, but the Oudegeests have, and things are going to improve," Bonds said.

Kees had been the assistant coach of the Dutch national team, one of the

> "We want a swimmer in the Olympics. That's why we hired Oudegeest. No other Arkansas coach has had Olympic experience, but the Oudegeests have, and things are going to improve."
>
> — John Bonds

> "I remember standing along poolside and hearing the U.S. national anthem played over and again as Americans won one gold medal after another. That's when I realized my future was in the United States."
>
> Kees Oudegeest

The swimming Oudegeests

Prior to moving to Little Rock in 1969, Coach Kees Oudegeest had built the Dutch National Team into a world swimming power and coached teams at three Olympics.

LRRC swimmers were motivated by his positive attitude and his sense of humor. A favorite Oudegeest saying: "My grandmother with a wooden leg could swim faster than you!"

Linda Frazier spoke of her new coach:

"One summer when I was 12 or 13, I was a teenager starting to smart off. I got kicked out of every practice. It made me mad. But Kees saw potential in me I didn't realize. Next year, when he sat me down at the beginning of the season to set goals, it was all mapped out for me. We did the practices and the times were marked off. It dawned on me that he knew what he was doing. I started working harder. I was 14 when I got my act together."

Assistant Coach Mary Kok Oudegeest had been a multiple world record holder, a professional distance swimmer, and a record-setting English Channel swimmer. She was inducted into the International Swimming Hall of Fame in 1980, where her citation states she was one of the most prolific world record holders (10 records in 1955) and one of the world's greatest marathon swimmers. Mary's photo shows an early type of swim goggles used by open water swimmers in the 1960s.

world's best in the 1950s, and head coach of the Spanish national team at the 1960 and 1964 Olympics.

"I remember standing along poolside and hearing the U.S. national anthem played over and again as Americans won one gold medal after another," Kees told the *Arkansas Democrat* in 1972. "That's when I realized my future was in the United States."

By 1967, Kees and Mary had emigrated to the U.S. After building a state champion swim team in the predominantly low-income community of East St. Louis, they were ready to move on. Kees was impressed by the private initiative that established the Racquet Club and the ambitious creed that guided its swimming program.

"I want an Olympic swimmer just like they do. There's a future for a coach in a club that has desire like that. It's fantastic."

Politics and Athletics

Mary Oudegeest had achieved international success before coming to Arkansas. But her swimming career, similar to the experiences of some Arkansas swimmers, demonstrates that politics and athletics are often a bad mix.

As a star of the Dutch team in the 1950s, she set the first of 10 world records when she was thirteen years old. In 1956, she had qualified to attend the Olympics in Melbourne Australia, but Dutch officials boycotted the Games.

At the 1971 Pan American Games in Cali, Columbia, Arkansas' first international champion, Pat Miles, came home with stories of the mysterious death of a Cuban athlete. Miles said the man had been beaten by the communist country's security guards and thrown from a building in a simulated suicide.

And in 1980, the U.S. boycott of the Moscow Olympics impacted several Arkansas swimmers. Among the many demoralized athletes who had qualified for the Olympic Trials were Randy Ensminger and Jerry Spencer, both attending the University of Arkansas. Bill Stafford, a Little Rock high school senior who was training that year in Nashville, TN, was another Olympic Trials qualifier. Stafford recalled that some American swimmers he trained with inquired about attending the Moscow Olympics on their own. They were informed by the State Department that their passports would be confiscated if that were attempted, Stafford said.

In 1960, Mary Oudegeest was again selected for The Netherlands' Olympic Team. But the 20-year old distance swimmer turned professional that year. She began open-water racing, winning a 25-mile race at Atlantic City, New Jersey and a 22-hour race in Argentina. In 1961, she was the first Dutch woman to swim the English Channel, setting a national record time of 12 hours 25 minutes.

In Little Rock in the 1970s, Mary was raising three children. She also worked as assistant coach at the Racquet Club and, in the 1980s, as head coach of a new program, the Central Arkansas Swim Team. She also competed in the new national program, US Masters Swimming, and the local Arkansas Masters Swim Club.

The Winning Combination

At the Racquet Club, the experienced coaching and local talent began to achieve results. Headlines about swimming in the 1950s and 1960s almost exclusively touted the Little Rock Boys Club. In the 1970s, praise for individual and team victories were virtually all focused on the Little Rock Racquet Club.

Dolphins win the AAU meet
The Arkansas AAU Age Group Outdoor Swimming Championship meet saw four meet records broken, and the Little Rock Dolphins emerge as the meet winners. The Dolphins, with 1,341 points, clearly outpointed their nearest opponent, the Little Rock YWCA, who totaled 577 points. In third was Miller Swim Gym with 478 points, and fourth was the Fayetteville Youth Center with 331 points.

Arkansas Democrat, July 24, 1972

Melissa Thompson, 15-years old in 1970, became the first woman from Arkansas to qualify for AAU Senior Nationals. Her time of 1:02.9 in the 100-meter freestyle was rated in the Top 25 in

Off to Dallas
Kees Oudegeest, Racquet Club swimming coach, with 14-year old Linda Frazier (center) and 17-year old Kathy Sullivan prior to their leaving for the 1972 National AAU Swimming Championships in Dallas. Linda, the youngest qualifier that Arkansas has sent to the Nationals, will compete in the 1,650-Yard Freestyle, and Kathy, making her third trip, will compete in the 100 and 200-Yard Freestyle events.

> "It was then I was proudest to have won for my country, for Arkansas, and for the Little Rock Racquet Club."
>
> Pat Miles

the world. Two years later, she qualified for the Olympic Trials in that event. Other top female swimmers—Kathy Sullivan, Autumn Buddenburg, Diane Letzig, Natalie Glover, Linda Frazier, and Karen Hight—were Senior National relay qualifiers and multiple state record holders.

Doug Martin and Pat Riley, Jr., were Racquet Club standouts on the boys' team. Both began swimming at the YMCA, then made great improvement under Dolphins coaches. And both won repeated media praise for setting state high school and AAU records. Martin was a gifted athlete who attended Vanderbilt University on a football scholarship, swam competitively, and played professional football for a year.

Riley completed his high school years as Dolphins team captain. Among other achievements, his come-from-behind, anchor-leg swim in the 400 Freestyle Relay in March 1973 gave the Dolphins its first Region 8 win. Riley swam and played water polo at Southern Methodist University.

Pan Am Gold

Local teenager Pat Miles was the first Arkansas swimmer to achieve international recognition. He did it by winning a gold medal at the 1971 Pan American Games.

As a 14-year old in 1967, Miles was already far ahead of local competition, setting national age group records in the 500-yard freestyle and 200-yard backstroke. Racing the mile in 1968 in Chicago, Miles was so far ahead of competitors, he was mistakenly stopped by officials two laps short of the 66-lap event. He completed the race, winning with a minute and a half lead over the second place swimmer.

In 1970, now coached by Oudegeest, Miles swam a 1500-Meter Freestyle in

Pat Miles displays his Pan American gold medal.

At His Proudest. *Pat Miles was greeted by more than 150 cheering fans at the Little Rock Airport when he returned from his victory in the 1500-Meter Freestyle at the 1971 Pan American Games.*

"It was then I was proudest to have won for my country, for Arkansas, and for the Little Rock Racquet Club," Miles later wrote in the team newsletter.

17:02.03, nearly twenty-three seconds below the national qualifying time, and a 400-Meter Freestyle in 4:16.4, nearly four seconds below the national qualifying time. That summer, the seventeen-year old Miles was world ranked with the 14th fastest mile swim in history and the 2nd fastest ever for his age group.

At the 1971 Pan Am Games, Miles, then an eighteen-year old freshman at Southern Illinois University, won the 1500-Meter Freestyle in a meet record time of 16:32.0. His time was twelve seconds faster than the old mark set by former world record holder Mike Burton.

Miles wrote about the experience in the September 1971 issue of *Bubble Babble*, the Dolphins swim team newsletter: "As I was going to the blocks, the whole team was yelling and shouting encouragement…All during my race, I could think of nothing but GOLD. I've never been more tired or happy after a race than when I finished and knew that I had won."

"A 15-Year Old Charmer"

Male sportswriters have occasionally been smitten by the smile and athletic grace of an ingénue. It happened in Little Rock in the 1940s when journalists swooned over teenage swimmer Sue Keith. It happened again in 1973, when the *Arkansas Democrat* profiled, world-ranked distance swimmer Linda Frazier.

"She walks into the Racquet Club dome swimming complex and all eyes turn her way. Even the smallest of tykes know who she is. There is that certain charisma about the teenager. And that ever present smile. She seems to shy away from publicity, but graciously puts up with it.

Her name is Linda Frazier, a petite 15-year-old charmer who is currently not only the top name in swimming at Little Rock but in Arkansas and the Southwest …"

Frazier qualified for AAU Senior Nationals in 1973 with a 17:24.27 in the 1650-Yard Freestyle, a 42-second improvement of her personal best. She was 8th in the nation and 10th in the world in the event.

Her first national qualifying time came when she was fourteen, the youngest Arkansas swimmer ever to qualify. She had been swimming and racing since she was four.

During her years as an honor student at Little Rock Hall High School, Frazier qualified for five national meets. Her distance training was often ten miles per day, requiring an hour or more before school at 5:30 a.m. and another two-to-three hours in the afternoon. No swim goggles were used in those years. Rubber strips from cut up bicycle tires secured a swimmer's ankles during pull sets.

Her teammates were in awe of her work ethic. So was the media, who did not fail to mention that none of the boys could keep up with her. Projections were often made of her Olympic potential, particularly after the 1972 Games when former Arkansan Keena Rothhammer won a gold medal in the 800-Meter Freestyle. Rothhammer and Frazier had been closely matched competitors in their 8 & Under years. Races ending in a tie, Frazier recalled, were resolved by an official flipping a coin.

To qualify for the 1976 Olympic Team, Frazier needed to maintain intense training for two years after high school. A scholarship offer from the University of Alabama and Olympic Swimming Coach Don Gambrill made that possible. But Frazier needed a change. She chose instead to attend the University of Arkansas at Little Rock and swim on a far less demanding level.

"I had given up a lot by that time, and I was tired," she said in a 2010 interview. "I met my future husband and was married at twenty."

National Age Group Top 5 Relay Team
Phil Mains, chair of the Arkansas AAU Aquatic Committee, presents awards to Linda Frazier (left), Autumn Buddenburg (center), and Diane Letzig (right) for the Dolphin team's recording the fifth best time in the country, 8:12.8, for the 800-Yard Freestyle Relay (15-17 year age group) in 1974. (Team member Kathy Sullivan is not shown)

> "I had given up a lot by that time, and I was tired. I met my future husband and was married at twenty."
>
> Linda Frazier Bland

What is the Difference Between Sprinters and Distance Swimmers?
"Sprinters are always lazy and have it easier than distance swimmers. It didn't seem fair to me that the national attention always seemed to be on them. And the mile is almost always the last event when people are packing up and ready to go. Sometimes they would say to me, 'Hurry up so we can get on the bus and go.'"

Linda Frazier Bland

"Any good swimmer out there who's willing to keep practicing can make all sorts of goals. Maybe not the Olympics, but achievement, even the smallest one, is what it is all about."

Kees Oudegeest

Arkansas High School Swimming

As the Dolphins' achievements increased, so did their team pride. When a local sportswriter suggested that the state high school swimming championship was Arkansas' top competitive venue, Dolphins swimmers took offense and sent the following letter, signed by 36 team members:

June 14, 1976
To Orville Henry, Sports Editor, *Arkansas Gazette*

This letter intends to educate the newspaper on the Arkansas high school swimming championship, which the Arkansas Gazette called "the premier swimming meet in the state." It should be understood that only 10% of state swimmers are involved in their high school teams, no Arkansas high school runs a swimming program, and that participants at the school championships have achieved their prowess as part of their AAU clubs.

Throughout the United States, the general sentiment about Arkansas is one of a backward and extremely slow state. Most of the swimmers on the Dolphins team have lived their whole lives in Arkansas and are extremely loyal to their home state.

We want to set this state straight on its picture of competitive swimming. There are thirty AAU meets held in one year in Arkansas, as opposed to one in high school. Our high school coaches are assigned to sponsor, not coach, swimming

99% of the swimmers in Arkansas are AAU swimmers, and they go virtually unnoticed. This is a great injustice to those athletes who put in three hours of training in the winter and four hours a day throughout the summer in strenuous exercise.

We average 13,000 meters a day in the summer, which is equivalent to 36 miles running. These athletes are more dedicated than the average high school athlete. All we ask for is fair representation in your news service.

Swimming in Arkansas is AAU, not high school, yet the high school meet is billed as the "premier" swim meet in the state and involves less than 10% of the swimmers in the state.

Sincerely,
The Little Rock Dolphins

Today, Frazier is a Little Rock realtor who maintains an active level of health and fitness for herself and her children. It's a lesson she learned from her parents about following through on a commitment. And the modest smile that once charmed a reporter can still be seen on her face.

Oudegeest put Frazier's choice in perspective stating, "Any good swimmer out there who's willing to keep practicing can make all sorts of goals. Maybe not the Olympics, but achievement, even the smallest one, is what it is all about."

A Tragic Loss

In 1974, the Arkansas swimming community suffered a tragic loss. Jimmy Miller died unexpectedly in March that year. He was 50 years old.

That summer, the Region 8 Long Course Championship was scheduled at the Racquet Club's new 50-meter pool. But a torrential rain storm just prior to the meet flooded the pool with a hillside of mud. Another site had to be secured to avoid cancellation of the meet.

"I got a late night call from one of our members about the Racquet Club wanting to use our pool," Boonie Miller said in a 2010 interview. "I thought it would be an honor to Jimmy to hold the meet here."

The July 1974 program was dedicated to Miller, and swimmers responded by swimming faster than ever before.

(Continued on page 62)

Man's Dreams Left Unfulfilled

By Orville Henry, *Arkansas Gazette*
May 29, 1974

Jimmy Miller's dreams always outstripped his means, wildly. The best dreams are like that. Jimmy did better than most of us. Many of his dreams came true. He just never got much of the cake. Hardly a piece.

This is how it started.

Coming out of the Air Force, Jimmy swam his way through to a degree at Northwestern Louisiana at Natchitoches, one of the first schools in the area to foster varsity aquatics. He landed at Little Rock as Athletic Director of the Boys Club. That meant he would spend a great deal of his time as babysitter (lifeguard) in the club's tiny basement pool.

That was the fall of 1949. A year later, age group swimming began to catch on across the country. To Jimmy, that meant one thing. The 5, 6, 7-year-olds splashing at his feet could become competitors.

It took Jimmy almost a decade to get age group swimming established in Arkansas. But he did.

Spread the Word

First, he spread the word. When he couldn't interest sports writers, he became one. Sort of. He submitted articles to this department, first awkwardly handwritten, then painfully typewritten, and finally good enough to print. He pleaded, cajoled, and berated the power structure: build us some pools. And later, as the Olympics on television laid it all out before his youngsters' eyes, some competitive pools. He organized meets, ran them off, typed the results, and delivered them to the presses. He made pilgrimages to Indianapolis, a swim capital, and Bartlesville, Oklahoma, where the Philips Oil Company was already switching an emphasis from men's basketball sponsorship to community participation programs. He came back and held clinics over the state, preaching development by age groups. (He practiced what he preached; his children usually could swim before they could walk.)

Jimmy left the Boys Club in 1959 to teach school, but he did not leave the swimming team. Nor did he give up his crusade. By 1968, he was ready to make the leap. On a piece of ground on Sam Peck Road off Highway 10, he built his own outdoor 50-meter pool, Olympic sized. He called it Miller's Swim Gym. He thought he could make a go of it, but a man without capital needs more than dedication and willingness to put in 18 hours a day to make a business enterprise succeed.

Age group swimming is the closest thing to the ideal of communal living one might imagine. The coach first meets the pupils when they are 3, 4, 5—all the way up to seven or eight. He is with them three-to-five hours a day, and at two or three different times a day. He is, perforce, with their parents, too. Parents must do far more than chauffeur. They time, they corral, they work the towels, they mesh into a family. It is amazing how well all the youngsters, all the parents, thrive happily together in this one year-round unending activity.

Gained Backers

So some of the swim parents stepped in as Jimmy's backers. Furthermore, last December, they opened a 25-yard indoor pool. They would pay the bills, not inconsiderable ones, and Jimmy would have a salary.

Jimmy never did anything halfway. When he suffered a coronary this past Sunday, it was a massive one. He died instantly, a youthful 50. He left a wife and eight children with no means of support.

The Miller Swim Gym's first outdoor meet is scheduled two weeks hence. His team members, including a 17-year-old who has been with the group for a dozen years, contend that the meet will be held on schedule. They will have the pool and the paperwork ready.

That's short-term. No one knows what the long-term will bring.

I thought of trying to explain what Jimmy meant to all these youngsters he's introduced to the water over the past 25 years. The picture says it best.

Jimmy Miller instructs a youngster in technique.

> "Jimmy always said this would be the fastest pool built. The kids set so many records that day, it brought joy to my heart for him. That was why he built the pool."
>
> Boonie Miller

Twenty-three meet records were broken, and thirteen swimmers qualified for Senior Nationals.

"Jimmy always said this would be the fastest pool built," Boonie Miller recalled. "The kids set so many records that day, it brought joy to my heart for him. That was why he built the pool."

Following Miller's death, the pools and site were sold to the West Little Rock YMCA. Predictably, the YMCA leadership was more interested in swim lessons and recreational aquatics than in competition. Only one lane was assigned for team training. Several of Miller's swimmers joined the Dolphins Team.

Governor David Pryor welcomed the Dolphin team at the State Capitol after its return from swimming in Venezuela. Team uniforms and other gear were provided by the West Little Rock Optimist Club, which won a national award for its sponsorship. In the photo: Robbin White (far left), Karen Hight (2nd from right), and Kees Oudegeest (right).

"The Dolphins in their Habitat" proclaimed the Venezuela newspaper headline when the Little Rock swimmers came to Caracas for the 1977 swim meet. Coach Robbin White (in white shorts) and former coach Kees Oudegeest look on from the deck. The poster at right was part of the local publicity.

Foreign Travels

In June 1973, Oudegeest received an invitation from the Spanish Swimming Federation for the Dolphins Team to compete in a series of swim meets and water polo matches.

The two-week trip to Spain was made by twenty-three Dolphin swimmers, coach Oudegeest, and several chaperones. Governor Dale Bumpers appointed the swimmers special goodwill ambassadors from Arkansas, and Senator J. William Fulbright issued them special dignitary status representing Arkansas and the US.

Competitions were held in Barcelona, Madrid, and other cities. Dolphins swimmers played water polo in the evenings against local teams. Mayors spoke at local meets, and the U.S. and Spanish national anthems were played. The trip concluded with a highly publicized meet in Madrid where the Spanish National Minister of Sports presented the Dolphins with an award.

Diaries and journals maintained by the swimmers recount the experience, the races and the long days. Many of the diary entries illustrate the Arkansas teenage swimmers' naiveté in international settings.

> "…the reception where the host team ate most of the food they offered. After the changing of gifts, I was obligated to kiss their captain when she turned her cheek."
> *Pat Riley, Jr.*

> "The nightclub food was quite good and the garlic was quite strong. The flamingo dancing was very interesting. I really enjoyed it."
> *Scott Bowen*
> NOTE: Bowen's journal incorrectly uses "flamingo" in place of "Flamenco."

> "There was a bottle of wine on the table for every meal. Also, at the receptions before the meets, the team would serve potato chips and wine."
> *Rick Witherspoon*

> "There was wine and cheese and sausage all set out right before you swam. I drank the wine. I got so sick I lost 20 pounds on that trip. All the food was soaked in olive oil."
> *Linda Frazier*

In 1977, the team made another international trip. Though no longer Dolphins coach, Oudegeest had once again leveraged his international connections to secure an invitation from the Swimming Federation of Venezuela. Some planning and correspondence was facilitated by Gustavo Sonoja, a Venezuelan college student studying in Little Rock and swimming with the Dolphins Team at the time. Upon their return, the Dolphins swimmers' were invited to the State Capitol for a reception hosted by Governor David Pryor.

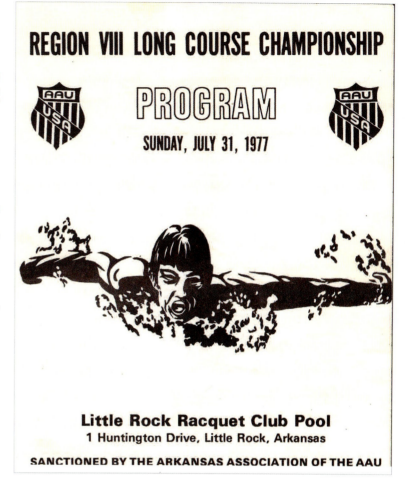

> "I was very much in fear that others would find out about me. I didn't know of any other gay swimmers and really had no one to talk to."
>
> Bill Stafford

New Coaches and New National Champions

Through the 1970s, the Dolphins had several new coaches, Bob Teichart in 1974 and Robbin White in 1976. In the summer of 1978, Sam Freas, the newly hired coach at the University of Arkansas, also worked as the Dolphins coach. Freas was assisted by Ken Kirchner, who would later be the UA head swim coach, and a young coach from West Virginia, Paul Blair. The three men spent the summer in the homes of Racquet Club members, with Freas traveling to Fayetteville on the weekends.

During this time, two new national champions emerged.

Bill Stafford: Coping with Intolerance

Bill Stafford began swimming as an eight-year old at the Miller Swim Gym and later the Little Rock Racquet Club. A nationally-ranked freestyler and individual medley specialist, Stafford relocated to Nashville in his senior year of high school to train with Olympian Tracy Caulkins.

Following the 1980 US boycott of the Olympics, Stafford competed for the University of Texas where he was a 12-time All American and a member of the NCAA championship team in 1981. For the next three years, Stafford won the 200-Yard Individual Medley at the Southwest Conference Swimming Championships, setting a new event record each year. In 1983, he had the fastest 200-Yard Individual Medley time in the nation and was chosen for the US National Team.

Stafford was a top contender for the 1984 Olympic Team, but a personal secret and an intolerant community stood in the way. Rumors had begun to circulate on the Austin campus with an article due to be published in the school newspaper about a gay swimmer who should be kicked off the team.

"I was very much in fear that others would find out about me," Stafford said. 'I didn't know of any other gay swimmers and really had no one to talk to."

Stafford shared his concerns with UT Swim Coach Ed Reese and offered to give up his swimming scholarship. Though Reese encouraged him to remain on the team, Stafford had a difficult time relating to his teammates.

"The toughest day for me was going back into the locker room knowing that

Bill Stafford *was the fastest 200-Yard Individual Medley swimmer in the nation when he attended the University of Texas in 1983.*

> **What is the Difference Between Sprinters and Distance Swimmers?**
> "Sprinters are fast and furious. Distance guys are slow to rise and 'steady as she goes.' They don't seem to ever get tired."
>
> **Bill Stafford**

the entire team knew I was gay," Stafford said. "I didn't know how to handle it. I quit swimming and school after my third Southwest Conference win and the following NCAA championships."

Looking back, Stafford said that decision remains the biggest regret of his athletic career. But like many athletes who learned discipline and goal setting from their sport, Stafford applied himself to a new endeavor. For the next fifteen years, he worked with a nonprofit performance organization, giving high-risk children a development path through theater.

When Stafford eventually returned to school, he obtained a nursing degree and worked as an Intensive Care Unit cardiac specialist. Today, he is a consultant to doctors for heart pump implants. He was inducted into the Arkansas Swimming Hall of Fame in 1991.

Randy Ensminger: Striving for Perfection

Randy Ensminger began taking swim lessons at the age of five from John Brooks. He joined the Little Rock Boys Club team and was coached by Jud Bryan and John Torbett. But it was Jimmy Miller who convinced Glenda Ensminger that her son had Olympic-level talent.

Ensminger said he was more interested in golf and tennis, but his parents switched him to the Miller Swim Gym. He recalled age group workouts in heavily chlorinated pools and weekend meets in the noise, and heat of the Little Rock YWCA. Numerous age group victories soon followed, but Ensminger wasn't thrilled with the sport.

"I would get sick and throw up before the races," he said. "That continued through college. I would go to the bathroom, throw up, then come back out and win."

Following Miller's death, Ensminger joined the Dolphins team. His attitude soon changed, as did the level of his achievements. As a senior at Little Rock Catholic High School, he won races at three Region 8 meets and qualified for

Randy Ensminger *was awarded the 1979 Neil Martin Victory Trophy as the top amateur athlete in Arkansas. Swimming for the University of Arkansas, Ensminger was on a 1981 team that set a world record of 3:22.33 in the 400 Meter (sc) Freestyle Relay. UA Coach Sam Freas proclaimed it "the greatest accomplishment in Arkansas swimming."*

> "I've got something against being second. If you want to be the best, there's nothing else but first."
>
> Randy Ensminger

three AAU Senior Nationals. He was a High School All-American for three years and was rated in the Top 20 in the US with a 52.3 for the 100-Yard Backstroke. In the process, he learned about striving for athletic perfection.

"I've got something against being second," Ensminger said. "If you want to be the best, there's nothing else but first."

In 1979, Ensminger was recognized as Arkansas' top amateur athlete with the Neil Martin Award. That year, Ensminger was the most recruited high school swimmer in the state, receiving more than thirty scholarship offers. He chose the University of Arkansas, where Coach Sam Freas was building a world class team.

"All my life I've wanted to be a Razorback," Ensminger said.

He was in fast company on Freas' UA team, racing with Jerry Spencer, who set a world record in the 50-Meter Freestyle, and British Olympian Martin Smith, who doubled as a place kicker for the Razorback football team. Smith became UA swim coach in 1985 and was later inducted into the Arkansas Swimming Hall of Fame.

Ensminger qualified for the US Olympic Trials in 1980 and 1984. He was an NCAA All-American in 1981 and UA team captain in 1983. In 1982, he was a member of the Arkansas 400-Meter Freestyle Relay that set a short course world record of 3:22.33.

Despite these accomplishments, Ensminger looks back on his swimming career with mixed feelings.

"I was never as good as I thought I should be," he said. "Swimming is so much more specialized now. I wish I had been a swimmer in the 90s, not the 1970s."

What is the Difference Between Sprinters and Distance Swimmers?
"Sprinters are spur-of-the-moment guys. Distance swimmers are prisoners of routine."
Randy Ensminger

Chapter 6. The Winning Formula: Parents

A Family Commitment of Support
The development of champion athletes requires far more than an individual's talent and drive. Swimmers and swimming families have identified two key factors that help explain championship performance. The first is the role of parents.

"Thank you so much for the wonderful weekend at the lake. You are so kind to take so many kids into your home and see that each one has a wonderful time. You outdid yourselves...I don't think I ever had so much fun in one weekend in all my life."
letter from Becky Heil to Liz Genz, June 1981

A thank-you letter from a child to a swim parent, such as the one Becky Heil wrote to Liz Genz, is a touching, though rare, acknowledgement. Like most kids, swimmers often don't recognize their parents' commitment and support until they are parents themselves.

At times, those supportive efforts can't be overlooked, such as the Rothhammer family's relocation in the 1960s from Little Rock to Houston and then to California to give 9-year old Keena the development path she needed to become an Olympic champion. In the 1990s, Manning Field benefited from a similar family commitment.

"My family moved to Little Rock so I could train with Paul Blair and the Racquet Club," Field, a Junior Nationals Qualifier with the Dolphins and Indiana University breaststroker, said. "The team helped me achieve my goal to be competitive on a national level."

Not many families can make such adjustments. More often, swimmers have been taken in by host families—sometimes for a summer season, sometimes for a school year. The sacrifices by parents, those who send their child away and those who open their homes to someone else's child, are considerable.

An extra swimmer at the table

For some households, an extra swimmer in the bedroom or at the breakfast table may not be a large burden. Kellie Stratton recalled the summers she and her sisters spent at the Little Rock home of Jimmy and Boonie Miller. The Pine Bluff girls were among the crowd of nine children raised by the Millers, most of whom swam on their father's team and trained in the family's small backyard pool.

No Rain Check
Judges Clell Callaway, Bryan Sims, and E.C. Miles weather the rains to serve as judges in the first Lakewood swimming meet that drew 350 entries in the first major outdoor swimming meet in Little Rock in recent years.
May 20, 1967

> "Parents see other parents involved, and it is easy to see why swimming is beneficial. At a meet, we officiate, we carpool, and we put up kids from out of town. We rely on others for help."
>
> Richard Turner

"Jimmy would come through the room and pull on our toes to wake us up for morning practice," Kellie recalled.

Mike Neuhofel of Conway was hosted by Little Rock families, a kindness he remembered some twenty years afterwards. He attributed that caring act to the family orientation of swimming.

Richard Turner, a 1960s-era swimmer at the Boys Club, agreed. "Parents see other parents involved, and it is easy to see why swimming is beneficial. At a meet, we officiate, we carpool, and we put up kids from out of town. We rely on others for help," Turner said.

Parents are commonly seen at swim meets working as timers, clerks, officials, hospitality hosts, and more. Rewards for that volunteerism are often nothing more than a morning of soggy shoes and the ringing in one's ears following a session of starter guns and screaming crowds. And in the excitement and congestion of age group swim meets, when children scurry about with events, heats, and lanes inked on their arms and legs, little attention is paid to those who supply the dry towels or to the thoughtfulness of hot meals waiting on the table long after the other members of the family have eaten.

Frank Letzig made many of those sacrifices in the 1960s when his three children swam for the Boys Club and the Racquet Club. Letzig was a senior swim meet official in Arkansas, but he also spent a lot of time in the mundane role of chauffer.

"I would get home, say hello to my wife, get my dinner in a sack," Letzig said. "Then I'd bring the kids to the pool, eat my dinner in the car and watch them work out. Quite a few parents did that."

Champions of Family Involvement

Parents stay involved as long as their children do. Liz and Terry Genz had more than a decade of active team participation, matching their son Tom's extensive years of success. And parents with more than one child swimming have a more extended involvement. The Stratton family had five daughters swimming. But the champions of family involvement have to be Jerry and Mary Heil and their nine children, all competitive swimmers.

The Heils moved to Little Rock in 1968 when Jerry was assigned the top state position with IBM. Anita Heil Parisi said her father, a successful high school and college athlete in Illinois, was committed to swimming because it included everyone and let all define their own levels of success.

"Mom liked swimming because we all came home clean and tired," Parisi said.

Parisi, an active swim coach in northwest Arkansas and mother of four age group swimming boys, remembered her father as a catalyst for advancing Arkansas swimming. Through his efforts, an IBM donation purchased the electronic timing system for state meets, she said. He also helped establish the Arkansas Swimming Hall of Fame, Parisi added.

The Heil house, with numerous bedrooms and a large yard, was able to absorb any number of swimmer guests, Mary Heil said. "Our house was always open to any swimmer. The beds and the floors were always full. They were all here together, not running around someplace we didn't know. It was great."

Located near the Racquet Club pools, the Heil house was also the scene of many pre-meet shave-down parties, Parisi said. "If there were nine or 24 kids there, it didn't bother my parents," she added.

Return on Investment

Communities invest in their youth through swim programs. Over the years, former swimmers influence their employers and civic organizations to sponsor swimming. In Little Rock, the return-on-investment can be seen in Dolphins team support from the West Little Rock Optimist Club, the investment firm, Stephens, Inc., and numerous local businesses.

Recognition programs have been established for special achievement, such as the "Heil Mile Award," given annually to Arkansas' top age group distance swimmers at the Arkansas Swimming Hall of Fame banquet.

Parent involvement *included smoking a cigarette while timing at a 1969 swim meet at Miller Swim Gym.*

> "It is the most wonderful thing to watch these kids grow up and become outstanding citizens and parents."
>
> Liz Genz

Eric Heil, a scholarship swimmer at the University of Arkansas, initiated the award in the 1990s. Though Eric was one of five Heil children that received athletic scholarships, Mary Heil had a realistic perspective on the award.

"Parents pay for those college scholarships before the kids receive them," she said. "Travel and meet costs add up. I am just happy we were able to do it."

Parents work as swim meet timers and officials. They assist in team fundraisers and banquets. They wake their children in the early morning darkness and bring them home well past a reasonable dinner hour. And some even give their children the chance to live elsewhere. All this is done because their children are engaged in swimming

"It is the most wonderful thing to watch these kids grow up and become outstanding citizens and parents," Liz Genz said.

What is the Difference Between Sprinters and Distance Swimmers?
"When the going gets tough, the sprinters put on fins."
Anita Heil Parisi

Chapter 7. 1980s

A Center Of Excellence In Swimming

The achievements of Little Rock swimmers in the 1980's, particularly the Dolphin men's team winning two Senior National Competitions, raised national awareness of Arkansas as a center of swimming excellence. The catalysts seemed to be the transcendent talent of swimmer Tom Genz and the inspirational coaching of Paul Blair. A host of other amazing talents, both homegrown and imported, followed in quick succession.

For Tom Genz, the 1980s was "a unique time of world-class swimmers."

Genz was one of the best of the nationally ranked swimmers who wore the Dolphins' green logo and were coached by Paul Blair at the Little Rock Racquet Club. But there were others like him: Arkansas teenagers and young adults, who won national titles, set national records, earned All-American status, and were selected to represent the U.S. at international competitions. Joining the Arkansans were recruited college swimmers, many of them world ranked, who benefited from the club's ambiance and dedication to athletic excellence.

In his early years as Racquet Club coach, Blair had shown that personal expectations and a team environment could motivate athletes to the highest levels of achievement.

"I believe you achieve to the level of what is around you. If you are surrounded by excellence and have a commitment to excellence, the result will be excellence. The best thing I can do for all my swimmers is convince them they can be better than they are and that they can swim faster than they think they can."
— Paul Blair

New Teams and Coaches

John Torbett was another swim coach who raised performance standards in central Arkansas. Torbett had been assistant director at the Boys Club and maintained the swim team following Jimmy Miller's departure in 1967. Under Torbett's leadership, the Central Arkansas Swim Team (CAST) was established in the 1970s. CAST combined the former YMCA, YWCA, and Boys Club teams and attracted new age group swimmers. Torbett, swimming coach at the University of Arkansas at Little Rock (UALR), provided the UALR pool as home base for CAST.

"UALR coach John Torbett changed my life. Some people come along in your life and do things you could never repay. That was Torbett to me. Much like Coach Blair, he looked to you to bring the passion to your sport. The more you brought, the more he would do. Torbett and Blair taught me that true greatness in competition comes from within. They taught me to be motivated about myself."
— Larry Golden, UALR and LRRC Dolphins Swimmer

One of the first CAST coaches was Rusty Wright, a UALR swimmer and water polo player. Prior to CAST, Wright had a

What is the Difference Between Sprinters and Distance Swimmers?
"Distance swimmers do it because they can't swim anything else. It's like taking your mom to the prom. You have no other choice."
— Tom Genz

"The best thing I can do for all my swimmers is convince them they can be better than they are and that they can swim faster than they think they can."
— Paul Blair

> "We were getting ready for the relays when a ceiling tile broke and a live raccoon fell down from the ceiling. It landed on my teammate George Thompson, scratched him, and then it ran out the open door."
>
> Tom Genz

brief coaching stint with a man he called his "mentor." In 1979, he was Paul Blair's first assistant coach at the Little Rock Racquet Club.

Wright, who is on the UALR health sciences faculty today, stayed with CAST until 1983. Following him, CAST was coached by Mary Oudegeest, who was replaced in 1986 by UALR All-American Kellie Stratton, one of five daughters, all competitive swimmers, from a Pine Bluff family. In 1990, Stratton would share coaching duties with two former CAST members and second generation Arkansas swimmers—Matt Torbett, 20, who started swimming at age four for CAST, and Angie Oudegeest, 21, a scholarship swimmer at UALR who swam for CAST when her mother coached there.

CAST provided a popular venue for age group swimmers. One of its early stars was 12-year old, Matt Twillie, a National Age Group Top 16 swimmer in three events in 1984. In 1987, CAST conducted its 15th annual Christmas Invitational meet at UALR.

The UALR pool, which had opened in 1970, may have been in disrepair as early as 1983 when an unexpected guest appeared at a district high school meet. Genz, a student at Little Rock Parkview High School, was on deck at the time.

"We were getting ready for the relays when a ceiling tile broke and a live raccoon fell down from the ceiling," Genz recalled. "It landed on my teammate George Thompson, scratched him, and then it ran out the open door."

The high school meet continued without further interruption, but the UALR aquatics building was marked for change. The building finally closed for renovation in 1992. Today, the facility is a modern student center with a state-of-the-art 50-meter indoor pool.

But CAST did not survive the interim period. The team disbanded when the UALR pool closed, and many of its top swimmers joined the Dolphins Team. Others joined a new team, the Little Rock Lasers, coached by Tay Stratton, a UALR Academic All-American swimmer and second-eldest of the five Stratton daughters. The Laser team had its home pool at

CAST Coach Rusty Wright *and swimmers at the Arkansas Age Group State Championship Meet, Little Rock Racquet Club, August 1982.*

the Little Rock Athletic Club, a private fitness center created by the Riley family in west Little Rock.

This changing scenario of teams and coaches did not adversely affect the swimmers. Instead, the new teams and new member families added to the growing environment of swimming excellence in central Arkansas.

Dolphins on the Rise

In 1983, newspaper headlines stated "Dolphins tell the nation they are on the rise" and "LRRC Dolphins dominate meet." But the Little Rock sportswriters occasionally were effusive in their praise. One news article that year began, "It's easy to remember when the Little Rock Racquet Club started a competitive swimming team. That's when swimming stopped being fun for everybody else."

The article intended to show the popularity of swimming in the state. A U.S. Swimming poll was cited, listing Arkansas as the fastest growing area in the country for competitive swimming. Since the 1960s, the article noted, Arkansas had progressed from a three-month summer season to year-round competitive programs with more than 900 registered age group swimmers and an increasing number of qualifiers for regional and national meets.

But Pat Riley, Sr., thought the article falsely suggested that the Racquet Club sought to diminish other swimming programs in state. In a letter to the *Arkansas Gazette*, Riley wrote that the club's intent was to move swimming and tennis to a competitive level of excellence and motivate the development of pools and swim programs across the state.

"This is what we really wanted," Riley's letter stated. "Sure, we wanted our team to come on and be good, but we wanted everyone else to follow along with us. This is so often the case—if you build something right—others for a while are stunned and then their competitive juices come into play and they start going out to compete."

In the newspaper article, Blair commented on the increasing number of teams and swimmers in Arkansas, stating, "when you get quantity, quality has to come somewhere along the line. Everyone's getting better and better, faster and faster." The influence of a world-ranked swimmer like Genz, Blair added, helped strengthen others like Eric Heil and Sande Southerland, and inspire young swimmers like Noel Strauss.

"When you hang around with guys like Genz, you start thinking fast," Blair stated.

Blair building swimmers, leaders

"We are one of the most unique teams in the country. We have more success on the national level with the fewest number than any in the country."

For Blair, success is more than what is measured in the pool; it includes the whole

Mike Booth (left) and Tom Genz model the new Hog Hat racing caps at a Region 8 Championship meet at Fayetteville, 1980.

Booth has been active in Arkansas swimming since he joined the Little Rock Boys Club team in 1974. He swam for UALR and the LRRC Dolphins, and he worked as assistant coach with the Dolphins and CAST teams. He started the Otter Creek Swim Team and has been a leader in creating the Central Arkansas Swim League, a community program with seven municipal teams and more than 800 swimmers. Booth has been a National Top 10 Masters Swimmer, and he serves on the board of directors of Arkansas Swimming, Inc. and the Arkansas Swimming Hall of Fame.

Dolphin team logo with the embedded #1, designed by swimmer Greg Bradley.

"When you hang around with guys like Genz, you start thinking fast."

Paul Blair

> "The best part of what I do is having some influence on youngsters—helping young people do their best, have fun, and swim fast."
>
> — Paul Blair

"Little Rock Racquet Club speeds to success in the fast lane under Blair's philosophy"
Arkansas Gazette, August 4, 1988

Paul Blair likes going fast.

"I get bored with things that take too long," he said. "That's why I like sprints."

The tanned, trim head swim coach at the Little Rock Racquet Club has been working hard lately to make his swimmers faster. The work has paid off. Eleven Dolphin swimmers have qualified for the U.S. Olympic Trials, and Blair's reputation for producing good sprinters is getting better all the time.

"I was a sprinter," he said. "I understand what sprinters need, and I'm good at training them. But the best part of what I do is having some influence on youngsters—helping young people do their best, have fun, and swim fast."

Blair is in his 10th year as head coach of the Dolphins. He was the only full-time coach the first six years.

Blair's hometown is Dover, Ohio. He started swimming when he was eight years old at the Dover YMCA and said he was the outstanding swimmer in every age group he competed in. As a senior at Dover High School, he was the state YMCA champion in the 50-yard free.

He swam two years at Ohio University. Freshmen were ineligible to compete for the varsity team, but as a sophomore he helped Ohio win the Mid-American Conference Championship. In 1971, he tranferred to West Liberty State College, a smaller school in West Virginia, where he was a two-time NAIA All-American. Blair started coaching as an assistant at West Liberty after his graduation in 1972. He coached at the Ohio Valley YMCA in Wheeling from 1972 to 1979. From 1973 and 1979, he doubled his duties coaching, working at Linsley Military Institute, a boys' private school in Wheeling.

"I took both teams from nothing to being 10th at YMCA Nationals and 10th at Prep School Nationals," he said.

Blair is a friend of Sam Freas, the Razorbacks swim coach from 1978 to 1985. In March 1979, Freas asked Blair to meet him and talk about another opportunity.

"Sam told me about a job at Little Rock and I said, 'Where's that?' Blair said. "He told me it was in Arkansas, and I said 'Arkansas?' I was skeptical. But he told me that it was a good opportunity, so I came down for an interview and got hired."

Now he's ambitious for the sport's success in Arkansas.

"It's such a great sport, and it does such good things," Blair said. "Swimming is the best all-around sport as far as conditioning and developing strength and flexibility. We need to convince the public that it could be a spectator sport."

"I'd love to see Arkansas have the best swimming in the country."

Future Champions
Paul Blair was well known for his national championship swimmers. The Little Rock coach was equally committed to the Dolphin's age group program. Over the years, assistant coaches Tom Genz, Bob Staab, Keith McAfee, and others helped Blair develop the character and athletic skills of hundreds of young swimmers.

individual. "They can't help but become a better person in our swim program," he said. "We encourage our athletes to become outstanding people and fast swimmers. If you want success you have to make it happen."

Blair, it seems, takes it as his responsibility to mold his athletes not only into excellent swimmers but into model young men and women.

"I like to refer to all my athletes as leaders," Blair said. "We try to teach all our kids to be leaders. And they do show and possess leadership qualities."

Arkansas Democrat, November 12, 1985

The Dolphins were rapidly outdistancing other swim clubs in Arkansas and elsewhere. LRRC swimmers' notable achievements in the period include:

March 1982, Region 8 Championships at Bartlesville, OK.
- 1st place in 400-Yard Freestyle Relay (3:09.9), and 400-Yard Medley Relay (3:30.26). [Larry Golden, Steve Claycomb, Mike Booth, Tom Genz]. The relay victories broke two eighteen-year old pool records set by Don Schollander and the Yale University team.
- Genz, 15, 1st place in 200-Yard Individual Medley (1:53.34)—fastest ever in the world for the age group.
- 1st place in Men's Division and 3rd place finish overall.

April 1985, McDonalds Junior Olympic National Championships, Milwaukee, WI.
- 2nd place in Men's Division with only five swimmers.
- Winner of 400-Yard Freestyle Relay (3:03.27), and 400-Yard Medley Relay (3:25.23) [Neil Bradley, Ricky Southerland, Sande Southerland, Mike Neuhofel]. Both relay victories set new meet records.
- Neuhofel, 1st place in 50-Yard Freestyle (20.6) and 100-Yard Freestyle (45.18).
- Eric Heil, 6th place in 1,650-Yard Freestyle (15:37.23).

Swimmers at LRRC make national Splash

"We wanted to show them how the boys from Arkansas can do it."

Sande Southerland

"Here we are a team with 90 kids from Little Rock, and we're able to put together the fastest relays in the country. There are other teams with 200 and 300 swimmers who can't put together relays equal to or better than ours."

Paul Blair
Arkansas Gazette, April 1985

Blair's coaching and the Dolphins' rising national stature attracted swimmers from other Arkansas teams. This trend was seen as early as 1982 at the state age group championship meet. The Dolphins took 66 swimmers to the meet, but eleven were listed as 'unattached' because they recently changed clubs.

Swimmers relocating to train with a coach or team of choice had happened before, but Arkansans generally left the state, as Keena Rothhammer did in the 1960s, to follow their dreams. Blair's achievements changed that.

Backstroker Neil Bradley qualified for the 1988 Olympic Trials and was a Senior National finalist in 1987. In 1984, Bradley had the fastest 100-Yard Backstroke in the nation (54.1) for 13-14 year olds. His time was the 2nd fastest ever for his age group.

> "People from all over country came to train here. They brought different talents that raised the bar for all of us."
>
> Mike Neuhofel

Some came from distant Arkansas towns, like brothers Steve and Scott Claycomb from Warren. Others came from nearby, like Mike Neuhofel from Conway or Anita Harrison from Jacksonville. Harrison said she recognized her need to change when, as a 15-year old, she was the sole CAST swimmer to attend the 1984 Junior Olympic National Championships.

> "In 1985, we took five guys and almost won Junior Nationals. We smoked everyone. A handful of people from Arkansas were kicking everyone's butt. That got national attention, and people began asking 'What is going on in Arkansas?' People from all over country came to train here. They brought different talents that raised the bar for all of us."
>
> Mike Neuhofel

Not every top Arkansas swimmer made the change. Jon Olsen of Jonesboro, a gold medalist in the 1992 and 1996 Olympics, swam for the Memphis State University age group team and the University of Alabama. And brothers Roy and David Gean took advantage of both worlds, training with the Dolphins in the summer yet keeping their affiliation with the Fort Smith Tideriders team through their successful age group years.

But others came from high schools and colleges around the country, especially in the Olympic years of 1988 and 1992. Little Rock swim families helped board the athletes, and Blair hired many of them as instructors in his summer programs. In 1989, he commented on the trend.

> "When I came here, I knew that to have a great swim team, I had to first get one swimmer to be great. Tom Genz was the first. Then there were two more, then four more, then junior national champions, then national level swimmers. Now I have world record holders calling me.

Fast women and shoulders of success—At left, Sandra Gattini, Nicole Reinhart, and Mindy Matheny (from left) led the Dolphins women's team in junior national qualifying times. Gattini qualified in the 200-Yard Butterfly, Reinhardt in the 50-Meter Freestyle and the 100- and 200-Yard Butterfly, and Matheny in the 50-Meter freestyle. At right, Tom Genz, 17th in the world in the 100-Meter Breaststroke, and Spanish Olympian Gustavo Torrijo (bottom, from left) shoulders Rick Southerland and Neil Bradley, both Junior National champs and members of record-breaking relay teams.
Arkansas Democrat, November 14, 1985

Innovation and Speed

Steve Crocker was among the top athletes that came to Little Rock in 1988 to train with Paul Blair and the Dolphins Team. A mechanical engineering graduate of the University of Kentucky, Crocker developed an innovative new concept for racing starts.

"I had done sketches of the human body and analyzed the forces at work—gravity and thrust," Crocker said. "When your event is the 50, there is a lot of incentive to work on starts. I came up with the 'catapult start,' a new way to give me that advantage."

Crocker said the existing "track start" put a swimmer's weight forward on the blocks and had both legs fire at the same time. His new technique was dominated by upper body forces. It involved grasping the edge of the starting block and leaning back, stretching the arms.

"You fire the back leg first, and your hands on the front of the block act as a hinge. As the hands release, you've converted leg power into forward speed," Crocker said. "The start is still being used today by a lot of top swimmers in the world."

For Neuhofel, the new start developed by Crocker, as well as the underwater streamline techniques introduced by Olympian David Berkhoff, ushered in a period of innovation.

"We weren't breaking rules, we were making new ones," Neuhofel said. "I vividly remember that transformation of swimming. It was an exciting time."

From left: Steve Crocker, Paul Blair, Doug Boyd—Nashville, TN, 1990

Dash for Cash

The idea of cash prizes for sprint racing was an experiment by US Swimming in the early 1990s. The "Dash for Cash" program invited sixteen top sprinters to a one-day, 50-freestyle tournament. Racing was one-on-one, every thirty minutes, with the winners advancing to the finals.

Doug Boyd and Steve Crocker were world-ranked sprinters who came to Little Rock in 1988 to train for the Olympic Trials. It was the "days of hired guns," Boyd said, a period when teams would provide incentives and support to draw top swimmers to their programs.

Boyd, current Swim Coach at Texas A&M, said Blair motivated athletes while developing friendships. "Not many can be a coach and a buddy at the same time," Boyd, said. "I learned from Paul how to keep my college kids motivated."

Crocker said his stroke improved due to Blair's persistence and daily modeling of the new technique. "Most coaches would have given up, but Paul knew I needed to be reminded over and over. He was the only person that would do that for me."

Crocker also developed a new racing start that made him the fastest 50 freestyler (short course meters) in the world in 1992. He set a world record that year at Dallas with a 21.64.

> "Early on, my parents were very involved, Dad as a meet director and Mom as a finish judge. When Robbin took us to the lake swims, Mom would cook for the whole team for the week-long program."
>
> Tom Genz

Tom Genz: The 10-year Old National Champion

Tom Genz set his first national age group record with a 33.7 for the 10 & Under 50-Yard Breaststroke in 1977. He would continue the amazing achievement for the next seven years, setting national records in four age groups.

"Tom is faster than any other ten-year old in history," Dolphins coach Robbin White said at the time. Six years later, Paul Blair was equally impressed, stating, "Tom may be the most talented swimmer today, anywhere."

Genz deserved the acclaim. In the early 1980s, he was the fastest-ever high school breaststroker and individual medley swimmer in the country. He represented the U.S. at international meets at home and abroad. He set Junior Olympic records, and he qualified for the Olympic Trials in 1988 and 1992.

He was a US Nationals Champion in 1985 and 1986. The first of those National titles came while he was a freshman at SMU. That spring semester, Genz was academically ineligible to compete for his school, but he trained on his own in Dallas. At the Los Angeles meet, he won the 100-Yard Breaststroke in 54.7 and the 200-Yard Breaststroke in 1:58.8.

Overall, Genz's outstanding career earned him the Arkansas Swimming Hall of Fame citation as "the premier swimmer of his time." But it was a career that almost ended well before its time when, as a fourteen-year old, Genz considered quitting the sport.

"Eat, swim, school—that's about all there's time for," Genz half-joked in a newspaper interview.

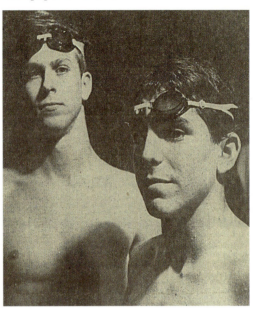

To Compete in National Meet
Tom Genz (right) and Scott Claycomb, representing the Little Rock Racquet Club, will be among five Arkansas swimmers competing in the United States Junior Olympic Swim Championships at Milwaukee.

Genz, 15, holds the fastest record in the country for 14-year olds in the 100-Yard Breaststroke with a time of 59.21. Claycomb, a junior at Catholic High School, broke the 10-year old Arkansas record in the 400-Yard Individual Medley, set by world-class swimmer Pat Miles.
Photo and caption: Arkansas Gazette, April 14, 1981

On the surface, Genz had the family support, team admiration, and respect of the entire Arkansas swimming community. Newspaper articles were lavish in their praise of his attitude, his achievements, and his home atmosphere. The Genz family helped find housing for out-of-town swimmers and for twenty years maintained a Thanksgiving Day tradition of swimmers dropping in to visit.

"Early on, my parents were very involved, Dad as a meet director and Mom as a finish judge," Genz said. "When Robbin took us to the lake swims, Mom would cook for the whole team for the week-long program."

A 1981 letter from former Dolphins swimmer Trip Strauss offered Genz further encouragement:

> "Since I quit swimming at the club, I've been concerned about the quality of the swimming program. I gave so much to it and got so much from it…I looked up to guys like Doug Martin and Pat Riley. It seems to me that you have emerged as your age group's link between my age group and the guys I respected. I like to think I held the torch for a while, then Ensminger and Stafford. Now it is yours. And Arkansas is a fine place to keep it lit. I just wanted to remind you that the older guys care where the team is going. Someday, when you look back, you will, too."

Genz started swimming at six years old when his family lived in Virginia. Two years later, they moved to Little Rock, and Tom was training with Jimmy Miller. Liz Genz, whom the affable Miller had nicknamed "Sunshine," recalled the coach's comment after her son's spectacular performance at an age group meet at Memphis.

"Jimmy said to me, 'Sunshine, we've created a monster,'" Liz said.

Miller did not live to see his swimming prodigy mature. Following Miller's death in 1974, Genz joined the Little Rock Racquet Club. He would soon be training four hours a day, six days a week.

"When Robbin White was coach, the team was every moment of your life. If you were sick, you sat in the bleachers. You never missed practice," Genz said. "Robbin's style of training included drawing charts and studying stroke and dive technique. We had to learn human anatomy, the bones and muscles, and there were written tests. For infractions, you had to write reports. One year, I was kicked off the team because of a time conflict when I played YMCA football. I had to petition to get back on."

Genz said the level of training and the sacrifices he made for the sport are difficult to comprehend today and might be considered abusive. But they were the norm at the time, and the talented Genz exceeded all expectations set for him. Despite his success, an inner tension was growing.

"I might have quit swimming at fourteen if Blair had not come along," Genz said.

Under Blair's coaching, Genz's time commitment and intensity of training did not change. Rather, Blair introduced a swimmer-coach relationship that gave Genz full responsibility for his actions. Blair helped Genz understand his personal goals and the effort needed to achieve them.

"The friendship of Paul and Tom was more than coach and swimmer," Liz Genz said. "Paul was an older brother for Tom, with a very healthy respect and caring on his part."

And like a caring older brother, Blair introduced Dolphins Team values that balanced "swim fast" with "be a good person" and "have a wholesome social life." In that environment, how someone performs on a college team or at the Olympic Trials is less important than an essential self analysis that asks, "Are you satisfied with your achievement? Did you fulfill your personal goals?"

The motivational atmosphere and coaching style changed for Genz at the right time in his development. It kept him in the sport for the remainder of his competitive years. His story offers an important lesson about how to avoid falling victim to one's own success and others' expectations.

Today, Genz lives in Little Rock with his family. He works as UALR Aquatics Coordinator at the Donaghey Student Center pool, a site replete with memories of a raccoon falling from the ceiling and years of age group swim meets. Genz says his job today is to fulfill the university mission to the community, including coordinating pool access for ten high school swim teams, summer league swim training, Dolphin-Lasers workouts, USA Swimming and high school meets, and open swim time for UALR students and staff.

The job seems a good fit. Like most everything he's done, Genz makes it look easy.

> "The friendship of Paul and Tom was more than coach and swimmer. Paul was an older brother for Tom, with a very healthy respect and caring on his part."
>
> Liz Genz

A Tale of Two Sprinters: Anita Harrison Henry and Mike Neuhofel

Anita Harrison Henry and Mike Neuhofel were co-recipients of the 1984 Gary Schultz Memorial Award. They both graduated high school in 1985—Henry from Jacksonville and Neuhofel from Conway—and that year both were listed among the Arkansas Gazette's "Arkansas Best High School Athletes." The newspaper wrote "Harrison was the fastest female swimmer to come out of Arkansas." Neuhofel was simply "the fastest high school sprinter ever to come out of Arkansas."

Anita Harrison Henry recalled her Dolphins years when she was "one of the guys," the only female fast enough to accompany Coach Blair and top sprinters Genz and Neuhofel to national and international meets.

In 1985, she was rated 13th in the U.S with a 23.4 in the 50-Yard Freestyle. Her 100-Yard Freestyle personal best time was 50.6. Henry was an eight-time All American at the University of Alabama, a self-defined "drop-dead sprinter" renowned for her anchor leg relay finishes.

She was also Arkansas' most accomplished high school violinist, seated first chair in the state youth symphony and frequently performing and traveling with the Arkansas Symphony Orchestra.

The former Team Captain at Alabama was twice voted "Most Inspiring" by her teammates, a response to what she called her passion for helping others. Those same qualities, she believes, continue to motivate her work as a mentor and life coach.

Some twenty years after her collegiate victories, she has completed an IronMan triathlon and is rated Top 10 in Masters Swimming backstroke events. "After the physical change of having three kids, I still always look for the next physical and mental challenge," Henry said.

Mike Neuhofel's imposing 6'6" stature is balanced by his disarming smile and welcoming handshake. Another self-described "drop-dead sprinter," Neuhofel was voted Captain of the US National Team in 1987, because, he said, "I had such a laid-back and friendly personal side but a very intense competitive side." Neuhofel was on the team for four years, swimming in two Pan American and two Pan Pacific Games. The ten-time All American at the University of Arkansas was a 50-Meter Freestyle silver medalist (22.7) at the 1987 Pan American Games and a member of the world's best 200-Meter Freestyle relay.

Conway's Bob Courtway, coach at Hendrix College and the Conway Aqua Kids, was Neuhofel's earliest inspiration. Paul Blair followed and opened up "a world of no limits," a combination of attention to detail and innovative ways of swimming fast. "It's not about swimming hard. It's about being efficient. That's what Paul Blair gave me."

Today, Neuhofel lives with his family in his home town of Conway. For some years, he provided leadership at the Boys and Girls Club and he's helped start a new team, the Central Arkansas Swim Club. Neuhofel remembers how his personal achievement was supported by his team, coach, and family.

"Swimming involves everyone around you who cares for you," he said. "I felt like I had to give back."

"An Attitude That You Are Going To Do Good"

Bob Staab, assistant coach for the Dolphins from 1985-1991, recalled a period in the mid 1980s when some 700 swimmers came to the Racquet Club for a Central Zone meet, when Noel Strauss was setting his first national age group records, and when ESPN came to Little Rock to tape a feature story on Kenyon Norman's breaking the 10 & Under record for the 50-Meter Butterfly.

"We had a good nucleus of kids," Staab said, "but it always came back to the 'Dolphin Difference.' Paul established that, and we kept preaching it. It was an attitude that you are going to do good."

"We had the whole package working at that time—a club whose creed was to develop top athletes, talented athletes working hard who wanted to succeed, and very capable parents with a positive attitude and a willingness to help. We also had big support from the West Little Rock Optimist Club and John Garrett. Our senior kids

> "We had a good nucleus of kids, but it always came back to the 'Dolphin Difference.' Paul established that, and we kept preaching it. It was an attitude that you are going to do good."
>
> Bob Staab

Matt Twillie, *17, had the fastest 100-Yard Butterfly in the nation (48.71) for 15-17 year olds and placed 5th at Short Course Nationals in 1989. Heavily recruited by top swimming colleges, he attended SMU where he became the first African-American champion in Southwest Conference swimming.*

Twillie was featured in a USA Today article ("Emerging Butterfly Star has big dreams waiting in wings," June 20, 1989), which noted his position as Captain of the West team at the Olympic Festival and his selection for a US team that competed in Russia in 1988.

As a 14-year old in 1986, he made his Senior National cut with a 50.24 in the 100-Yard Butterfly, fastest in the country that year for the age group and just .2 seconds off the national age group record.

Dolphins at the 1985 Junior Nationals. *Coach Paul Blair, Neil Bradley, Mike Neuhofel, Rick Southerland, Nicole Reinhart, Sandra Gattini, Mindy Matheny, Sande Southerland, Eric Heil.*

"There was a certain mystique of being on the senior team and working with the top coach. But Paul and I were there with all the development groups."

— Bob Staab

Eleven LRRC swimmers qualify for the U.S. Olympic Trials, August 8-13, 1988, University of Texas at Austin

Swimmer profiles from *Arkansas Gazette*, August 4, 1988.

50 Freestyle
- **Doug Boyd**, 23, of Prides Crossing, MA. A three-time All-American at Indiana University, he was ranked 29th in the world in the 50-Meter Freestyle in 1987 and is in the Top 15 in the U.S. with a personal best of 23.0.
- **Mindy Matheny**, 18, of Little Rock. She was 5th in the 50-Meter Freestyle in the 1987 National Age Group Championships and was chosen for the 1987 Olympic Festival Team. She was a member of the All-American Medley Relay team at the University of Nebraska.
- **Dan Powell**, 23, of Bowling Green, KY.
- **Noel Strauss**, 15, of Little Rock. He will be the youngest male swimmer at the meet.
- **Mike Neuhofel**, 21, of Conway. He has been an All-American at the University of Arkansas in seven events. He was a silver medalist in the 50-Meter Freestyle (22.84) at the 1987 Pan American Games.
- **Steve Crocker**, 25, of Franklin, KY. He qualified for the 1984 Trials in the 100-Meter Butterfly. He was an All-American at Western Kentucky State University, 2nd in the 50-Meter Freestyle at 1987 US Open, and 3rd at the 1988 Senior Nationals.
- **Nancy Duncan**, 20, of Arkadelphia. She is an All-American in 400-Yard Freestyle Relay at the University of Arkansas. She was 7th in National Age Group listings in 1987.

400 Freestyle
- **Eric Heil**, 21, of Little Rock.

100 Breaststroke
- **Tom Genz**, 22, of Little Rock.

100 Backstroke
- **Neil Bradley**, 19, of Little Rock. University of Arkansas swimmer.
- **Dave McCrary**, 20, of St. Louis, MO. In 1988, he was 2nd in the Southwest Conference and 16th in NCAA for University of Arkansas.

worked at the neighborhood pools and recruited for the summer leagues."

Staab said Blair had established a comprehensive program that offered swimmers a consistency across all age groups from swim lessons to pre-competitive development stages to senior levels.

"All kids heard the same catch phrases, all got the same messages," Staab said. "There was a certain mystique of being on the senior team and working with the top coach. But Paul and I were there with all the development groups."

"When the kids were with us, they worked hard and were willing to put in time and effort to make Regional and Junior cuts," Staab said. "A mind set had been established of reaching higher levels. They saw others doing it and they wanted that. It was expected that you would succeed."

High Drama and Victory

At the Phillips 66/USS Short Course Nationals in March 1989, the last event of the meet was a moment of high drama. Overall, the Dolphin team was only three points ahead of the Santa Clara Swim Club. Whichever team scored higher in the 400-Yard Medley Relay would win the Men's Division title. The Dolphins beat Santa Clara in the race but were disqualified for a relay false start. For a moment, it seemed Santa Clara had won the Men's title. But the Santa Clara team had also

Noel Strauss, the fastest young freestyler in America
by Trip Strauss (no relation to Noel Strauss)

Little Rock, 1988—Last summer at the Junior Olympic Championships for 18-year-olds and under in Mission Viejo, California, Noel Strauss won the 100-Meter Freestyle event in 51.59 seconds—setting the national record for 13-14 year olds by over two seconds. That is a phenomenal margin of victory in a race that takes only about as long to complete as track's 440-yard dash. The year before at the same championships, Strauss had won the 50-Meter Freestyle as a 13-year old—the first time a 13-year old had even qualified for the finals.

Strauss turned fifteen on August 30, and two months later in Orlando, Florida at the US Open Championships (for swimmers of all ages) he lowered his 100-meter freestyle best to 51.42 and went 23.25 in the 50 to shatter the 15-16-year-old American record in that event by two tenths of a second. It didn't go unnoticed by swimming fans that the age group record had belonged to Tom Jager, the current world-record holder in swimming's glamour race.

To put Strauss' accomplishments into even finer perspective, at the age of 15 he is swimming faster than any 16-year-old American ever has.

Strauss is without question among the most naturally talented sprinters America has ever seen. His stroke is reminiscent of that of Olympians Don Schollander and Mark Spitz. Dark complected and sleek, he even looks a lot like Spitz. Like all truly great sprinters, Strauss glides atop the water effortlessly, aided by a six-beat kick that could pull a couple of water skiers.

—Staff photo by Jeff Bowen

All Time Top 100 List
Dolphin swimmers have set many National Age Group records over the years, but only one remains unbroken. Noel Strauss (shown here in 1988) has two listings on the All Time Top 100 List of US Swimming, both set in 1987 when he was 14 years old. His time of 51.59 in the 100-Meter Freestyle remains the fastest ever swum for the 13-14 age group. His time of 23.81 for the 50-Meter Freestyle is the 2nd fastest ever swum for the age group and event.

Between 1981 and 1990, the LRRC had thirty four National Age Group champions. Strauss has accounted for seventeen of those.

What is the Difference Between Sprinters and Distance Swimmers?
"Sprinting is more of the glamour side. Sprinting is how fast you can go, and distance is how much pain you can endure."
Noel Strauss

> **What is the Difference Between Sprinters and Distance Swimmers?**
> "One's cerebral. The other's a maniac. One's cerebral. The other can't afford to be."
> **Sam Freas**

false started and was disqualified. In two quick swings of emotion, the Dolphins maintained their narrow advantage in overall points and won the Men's Division.

Other team accomplishments at the meet included:
400-Yard Freestyle Relay:
 1st - Steve Crocker, Doug Boyd, Matt Twillie, Noel Strauss (2:57.17)
50-Yard Freestyle:
 1st - Steve Crocker, (19.52)
 4th - Doug Boyd, (19.96)
100-Yard Freestyle:
 2nd - Doug Boyd, (44.04)
 6th - Steve Crocker, (44.51)
100-Yard Butterfly:
 5th - Matt Twillie, (48.74)
100-Yard Breaststroke:
 7th - Tom Genz, (55.85)

Additional Dolphin achievements, 1988-1989
- Steve Crocker, 3rd in 50-Meter Freestyle at Olympic Trials. Ranked 6th in world. Named to US National Team and US All-American Team.
- Doug Boyd, 9th in 50-Meter Freestyle and 7th in 100-Meter Freestyle at Olympic Trials. Named to US All-American Team.
- Mike Neuhofel, 7th in 50-Meter Freestyle at Olympic Trials. Named to US All-American Team.
- Paul Blair selected for National Swim Team coaching staff.

Mike Neuhofel training at the LRRC 50-meter pool for the 1988 Olympic Trials.

Age Group Swimmers named to Academic All-American Team
- Noel Strauss, 16, National Age Group champion in 50-Meter Freestyle (23.25, new national record) and 100-Meter Freestyle
- Matt Twillie, 16, National Age Group ranking 5th in 50-Meter Freestyle, 7th in 100-Meter Butterfly
- Basil Hicks, 14, National Age Group ranking in 6 events

> **Are Swimmers Smarter Than Other Athletes?**
> "Swimming teaches you a lot about setting and achieving personal and goals and improving by measurable increments. Those were always very appealing to me—what were my splits, what kind of drop off do I need to have. There are a lot of numbers involved."
> **Noel Strauss**

Little Rock, Big Success
Excerpt from June 1989 *Swimming World* article by Sandra Todd.

How was it possible that the winning team at the 1988 US Open and 1989 Short Course Senior Nationals, two of the most prominent competitions in the nation, came from one of the smallest LSCs in the nation? [LSC (Local Swim Committee): a regional grouping of swim clubs by USA Swimming.]

"I wasn't a coach who was a dictator or yelled or anything else," Blair said. "I slowly and methodically went about developing our program. Some people didn't think I was a very good coach because I was low-keyed. My approach was not to take over and siege. My approach was to work from within the system to nurture, educate, and develop a power base of support."

One hundred fifteen swimmers may not sound like a big team, but considering the sixty members Blair started with, Little Rock's membership is respectable. The fact that they've won national titles is practically unbelievable.

Over the past decade, Dolphins have claimed six US national gold medals, eight National Junior

Olympic championships, 27 national age group winners, and four swimmers who have set 16 National Age Group records. In 1984, one swimmer qualified for Olympic trials. In 1988, the Dolphins sent eleven swimmers to the Trials. Only four teams in nation had a larger number of Trials qualifiers.

His persuasive powers are strong, and most of the time subtle.

"Coaching is a great deal more than just training swimmers and going to competitions. It's a way of life. The key to our service is coaching kids and servicing their needs as well as their parents'. I sell a service—which is offering kids an opportunity to grow, mature, and develop as young people, as well as swim fast. Some kids are never going to swim fast, but they are going to learn a heck of a lot on the way.

Dolphins team priorities are 1. Academics, 2. Swim Fast, and 3. Wholesome Social Life. With those in mind, it's real simple and easy to have a good swim team. With those goals and priorities, people understand where we're coming from. It's the foundation or basis for our total program."

Noel Strauss: "Coach Blair doesn't make you do things, but he makes you think about what you are doing. He has always promoted individualism. He allows us freedom, so we're not rebel-

Bob Staab, Dolphin Assistant Coach, and Paul Blair, 1990

lious. I think he knows that we do things better if they come from within us."

Matt Twillie: "Coach is notorious for giving us motivational-inspirational speeches, and you get a new one every day."

Blair is famous as a sprint coach. In the two big meet wins in 1988 and 1989, no Dolphins swimmer scored in an event longer than 100 yards or meters. At the US Open, LRRC dominated the 50-Meter Freestyle, with Steve Crocker, 25, winning (22.74), Boyd, 24, 3rd (23.10), and Strauss, 8th (23.74). In the 100-Meter Freestyle, Boyd was 4th (51.19), Strauss was 7th (51.74), and Crocker was 10th (51.96). Twillie was 12th in 100-Meter Butterfly. The LRRC team was 2nd in 400-Meter Freestyle Relay.

"Because we're sprint based, the misconception is widespread that we don't do anything over 50s and 200s," Blair said. "We use a training cycle that I've been refining. We've gotten some good results from it. Steve Crocker came here in January 1988 at 22.91 in the 50. Within eight months, he went 22.65 and missed the Olympic team by 15-hundreths."

Blair explained the team workout schedule.

"They know which days high intensity workouts occur. The person we're trying to reach is the person who gears himself up and gets ready for the set or the days for the high intensity sets. It allows them to know what they're doing. They know what to expect."

Following the 1988 wins, Blair was offered the head swim coach position at the University of Arkansas. He chose to stay in Little Rock because the program future here is entirely his to control.

"Whatever we try to do, whatever success we have, it's because of us, because of our swimmers, parents, community, coaching staff and our club. We've done it …. We've developed that ourselves, and that makes us feel pretty good."

> "Coach Blair doesn't make you do things, but he makes you think about what you are doing. He has always promoted individualism. He allows us freedom, so we're not rebellious. I think he knows that we do things better if they come from within us."
>
> Noel Strauss

Blair's workouts emphasize quality rather than quantity. While some California teams crank out 15,000 to 17,000 meters a day, Blair's distance swimmers rarely train over 10,000 meters a day.

"The thing I try to do most of all," Blair explains, "is to treat athletes more like race horses than like plow horses. The basic philosophy of the program is it's not how far you can swim, it's how fast you can swim."

Excerpt from "Lightning Fast in Little Rock" by Trip Strauss

Sprint training system strives for top effort
Arkansas Gazette, August 4, 1988

Coach Blair's training for sprinters is an exact science. The 18-week, five-phase program is designed to develop free energy systems. Its objective is to bring the swimmer to his peak performance level for a specific day of competition.

"We backed up 18 weeks from when the Olympic Trials will be and started a program consisting of a four 4-weeks phases and a 2-week tapering phase," Blair said. He explained the three energy systems.

The first one is the ATP-CP system, an athlete's maximum explosive power that lasts only ten seconds. The second is an anaerobic system, which takes over after ten seconds and lasts up to two minutes. The third is the aerobic system, which kicks in after about two minutes and carries the athletes through the long haul.

"We developed these energy systems with specific swim workouts and dry land workouts [weight lifting]," Blair said.

Phase 1
The first four weeks is the aerobic training phase. It develops the athletes base level conditioning with distance swimming at 70% of maximum power output. Two hours a day, six days a week, the swimmer swims 6,000 to 7,000 meters, about 4 miles, with several short rests.

They start developing the ATP-CP system with short sprints that last five or six seconds, resting very briefly between.

On weights, the swimmers work almost all muscles on Nautilus or Universal systems, with slow repetitions concentrating on proper technique. They do one set of 20 light reps or warm-up and two sets of 10 heavy reps.

Phase 2
This is the threshold phase for working on the aerobic system. The swimmers do shorter runs at a faster pace, about 85% of maximum power, with short rests. They swim 4,000 meters per day, alternating between different types of sets. One day they'll swim ten 400-meter sets with 20 or 30 seconds rest between each set. The next day they'll swim four 100-meter sets with very short rest between. On the third day they'll swim four 1,000-meter sets and then repeat the cycle for the rest of the week. On weights they do one set of 10 light reps for warm-up, one set of 20 hard reps and one set of 10 maximum power reps.

Phase 3
Training in this phase is done at maximum speed for developing the ATP-CP energy system. The swimmers do shorter runs with their longer rest, about 2,000 meters per day of equal swimming and resting. They do mostly 50- and 100-meter sprints, and some 200-meter sets.

On weights, they do one set of 10 light reps and two sets of 10 heavy reps.

Phase 4
Blair calls this the "race-pace" phase. It's high-quality swimming at maximum power with lots of rest. It gradually decreases from 4,000-meter workouts the first week to 2,500-meter workouts the fourth week.

"We work hard on technique during this phase," Blair said. "I watch everything a swimmer does from the moment his little finger goes into the water to when it comes back out after the stroke. Technique is the most important aspect of the sport."

Weight training is done only during the first two weeks of this phase.

Phase 5
This is a two-week taper phase, for gradually letting the muscles recover from the breakdown phases of hard work. Day by day, the swimmers do less swimming and more resting. On the last day of this phase, the day before competition, the workout consists of merely getting in the water and working on stroke technique a little.

Chapter 8. 1990s

A Showcase Of Talent
A cadre of top high school and college swimmers continued to bring national attention to the Dolphins program. Foremost among these was the remarkable accomplishment of John Hargis, a gold medal winner at the 1996 Olympics. Through a combination of personal commitment, family support, and effective coaching, Hargis' success fulfilled the original creed of the Little Rock Racquet Club to produce world class athletes.

"The atmosphere was fun, but there was always a sense of awe. Within our small team we had some real national leaders—Strauss, Hicks, Twillie. These guys were the best in the country. To train with them everyday was incredible."
— Manning Field

Through the 1990s, the Dolphins Team continued to produce top swimmers and impressive results. Blair had the right ingredients for success—phenomenal facilities, a broad development program for younger athletes, and unique team camaraderie.

"The Dolphins knew what they wanted to achieve," Amy Gruber Burgess said. "Coach Blair was very good at setting that tone for getting down to business, pulling out the best in people, and getting them to work hard."

In 1990, four Dolphins were ranked by *Swimming World* magazine in the National Top 16. Leading the group was seventeen-year old Matt Twillie, whose 48.79 in the 100-Yard Butterfly was 2nd fastest in the nation that year. Noel Strauss, at sixteen years old, was listed in the 50, 100, and 200 freestyle.

In 1991, three Dolphins were named as Academic All-Americans by U.S. Swimming: Lindsey McVey of Lakeside High School, Hot Springs; Manning Field, freshman at Indiana University and Central High School graduate; and Jonathan Kletzel, Central High School, Little Rock. The award required a Junior National qualifying time and a minimum 3.5 grade point average.

Also in 1991, the local media discovered Priscilla Jones. In much the same way Linda Frazier generated attention twenty years earlier, another successful teenage girl became the spokesperson for her team's work ethic and goals. Having qualified for Junior Nationals that year, Jones attended a four-day camp at the U.S. Olympic Training Center at Colorado Springs.

Jones takes her swimming seriously
"Most athletes who are serious, if they

Manning Field

"The Dolphins knew what they wanted to achieve. Coach Blair was very good at setting that tone for getting down to business, pulling out the best in people, and getting them to work hard."
— Amy Gruber Burgess

Are Swimmers Smarter Than Other Athletes?
"On the average, they probably are smarter, but I've known many a dumb swimmer."
— **Manning Field**

> "I remember the Thanksgiving meet when we learned we wouldn't be there anymore. The emotional impact of losing your home was a shock, a big deal."
>
> Matt Weghorst

want to go anywhere, they have to be focused. This is what I want to do," Jones said. The 15-year old Central High School sophomore maintains a 3.68 GPA. She started swimming in a West Little Rock Optimist Club summer league program, joined CAST, and then switched to the Dolphins. "This is where I showed the most improvement and got the most support."

Arkansas Democrat, December 12, 1990

Club and Pool Changes

In 1995, four new Dolphins age group swimmers were ranked in the National Top 16. Leading this group was John Hicks, who, like his older brother Basil, excelled in distance events. John was rated 4th in the nation in the 13-14 age group in the 1650 Free that year.

1992-1993 Age Group Swimmers of the Year. *Back row: Matt Weghorst, Chris Sheppard, Betsy Harding, Shawna Blair, John Hicks. Front row: Lindann Blair, Paul Peavey, Katheryn Holt, Daniel Pupkowski.*

8 & Under Pride: *Lindann Blair, Daniel Pupkowski, Hannah Bakke, Harding College, Searcy, 1992*

The kids were still swimming fast, but the Little Rock Racquet Club was suffering from a declining membership and mounting financial difficulties. As a cost saving effort in December 1997, the Racquet Club board decided to no longer sponsor a swim team.

Losing their home pool was a challenge for the Dolphins Team. Matt Weghorst was a high school senior at the time. He had grown up at the club. He considered it and the Dolphins Team as home.

"I remember the Thanksgiving meet when we learned we wouldn't be there anymore," Weghorst said. "The emotional impact of losing your home was a shock, a big deal."

The swimmers never lost confidence they would find a place to train, Weghorst added. And Blair made sure things did improve.

He arranged for the team's summer training at the Westside YMCA 50-meter pool, originally built in 1969 for the Miller Swim Gym. The pool was only available in the early morning, so Blair arranged afternoon pool time for Dolphins workouts at UALR. Blair would soon accept the Assistant Head Swimming Coach position at UALR. For a few years in the 2000s, stability returned to the Dolphins Team as Blair coached both the club and the college squads.

At the Racquet Club, however, more changes were to come.

In the late 1990s, the club experienced a steady decrease in membership. Repairs and maintenance lapsed and challenging financial issues ensued. In 1999, the Racquet Club's board approached Riley's Health and Fitness Center (RHFC), now managed by Pat Riley, Jr., to consider a merger or sale. Membership of the Racquet Club voted in favor of a sale, which was completed late that year. In 2000, renovation on the old clubhouse and pools began. Under new management, the LRRC has returned to solvency, growth, and a renewed commitment to competitive swimming.

What is the Difference Between Sprinters and Distance Swimmers?
"You might be more introverted to swim distance. But as the saying goes, 'no brain, no pain.'"

Brent Peterson

Swimmer Profiles from the Dolphins Newsletter, September-December 1991

Jonathan Kletzel

Jonathan Kletzel will probably remember this past summer's Junior National Championships for some time to come. It was at the Mission Viejo California meet that Jonathan had life-time best times in four events, including a speedy 51.44 seconds for his freestyle leg of the 400-Meter Medley Relay.

"All my resting, all my tapering really came together," he said. "The timing was right."

Having competed in four junior national championships, Jonathan said he has gone beyond most of his early goals for swimming. "But as I've been achieving those, other goals have been extended. Athletically, I'm satisfied, but I'd still like to go for more," he said.

An 18-year-old senior and academic All-American at Little Rock Central High School, Jonathan has seen his times steadily drop and his dedication to swimming grow increasingly stronger in the seven years he has been a member of the Dolphins Team. He said a key advantage of the Dolphins Team was its variety of people, a factor that has encouraged him as an individual swimmer to make the most of pool time and feedback from the coach.

This year, Jonathan faces a new challenge. He has chosen to remain in Little Rock and swim with the Dolphins team even though his family has relocated to Chicago. While he'll see less of his family this year than he would prefer, Jonathan doesn't believe his swimming or his motivation will suffer.

Lindsey McVey

Lindsey McVey scoring her highest ever as a Dolphins swimmer at the Junior National Championships with a fourth-place finish in the 100-Meter Breaststroke, was somewhat philosophical about her lifetime best time of 1:15.35.

"If I could do it all over, I would have come here a lot sooner," she said, referring to her three years of training with the Dolphins. "The team here is like a family. Everyone lets you know they're behind you. They'll cheer you on even if your race wasn't your best."

Having to travel approximately three hours each day to attend practice, Lindsey has learned to discipline herself and focus on specific goals. Though she joins the team for afternoon practice, the 16-year-old junior from Hot Springs works out on her own in the morning. She has also abandoned basketball and cheerleading to focus solely on swim-

1989-1990 Outstanding Swimmers: *Matt Twillie, Priscilla Jones (right front). Most Improved: Lindsey McVey, Jonathan Kletzel.*

ming. But the team spirit she finds on the Dolphins team has compensated for the sacrifices, she believes.

"I worked all this time and improved so much, the motivation comes from inside me now," Lindsey said.

The advantage of training with the Dolphins team is both in the team spirit and the coaching, she said. "Coach Blair really works individually. He knows what you can do, and he lets you know it, too. He tells you exactly what you need to work on," she said.

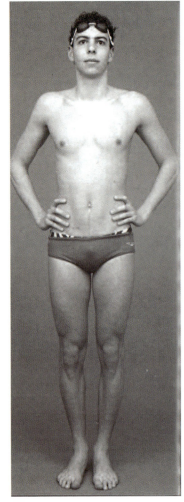

Central High School yearbook, 1992 Jonathan Kletzel
Named for his athletic achievements ... three-year letterman on Tiger swim team ... state champion in 100-yard freestyle event all three years in high school ... state champion in 50-yard freestyle in both sophomore and senior years ... ranked nationally in swimming ... named to the 1991 Academic All-American team by U.S. Swimming ... recruited by many college and university swim teams ... an honor roll student ... active in affairs of several clubs.

1996-1997 Most Improved: *Michelle Maguire, Matt Weghorst, Amy Gruber*

1993-1994 Outstanding Swimmers: *Scott Strauss, Kelly Wilson.* **Most Improved:** *Betsy Harding, Amie Marshall*

Paul Blair, a quiet competence

"Coach Blair lined you up to race other guys in practice. The biggest thing about being on the Dolphins was the competition. Every practice was basically a swim meet. You always had someone to race."

Matt Twillie

To David Guthrie, Paul Blair's coaching style was more of a partnership than a parental authority figure or Marine drill sergeant, more pulling than pushing. "He showed you that to get great results, you had to work hard, but he always communicated how you had to take responsibility and find it in yourself to do it." Guthrie said.

He remembered Blair as always focused and never upset, exhibiting a quiet power.

"One of his real gifts was calmness," Guthrie said. "A quiet confidence is what swimmers need to perform their best at big pressure meets, and a coach has more influence on that than anyone else. Paul's inspiration was not through external pressure. He got us to do it. We were motivating ourselves."

Blair's coaching style required a personal motivation. Top swimmers have this maturity. But Blair communicated this message across all age groups and skill levels on the Dolphins team. It was a foundation for the team motto "Believe in the Dolphin Difference." For Basil Hicks, it was a means for a team member to build individual drive and focus.

"Coach would communicate to you 'This is what you need to be better, and this is what I expect you to do.'" Hicks said. "The guys we swam with made that the currency. It was your choice if you would be a good swimmer or just hold your place."

"Coach lived for swimming, and he lived to see his swimmers excel and do well. His philosophy was: If you had your head screwed on right and you worked hard, you could accomplish anything."

Noel Strauss

A Personality-Driven Program

Blair's personality was shown in subtle ways, rarely raising his voice at a meet or practice unless a close race drew out an encouraging shout. Sometimes he paced the deck, sweeping his arm to signal a swimmer for more speed. But his relaxed demeanor, for the most part, was sufficient to communicate the intensity his swimmers knew was expected.

Blair's message to Arkansas swimmers was strong and persuasive, observed Dolphins swim parent Rick Field. Through a relaxed but intense approach, he got superior performances from all Dolphins age groups and created national champions. Maintaining a comprehensive team approach meant communicating possibilities to the Dolphins swim families,

Paul Blair, Sean Casey, Kelly Wilson, John Hicks.

something Blair excelled at, Richard Turner added.

"You need a great coach like Paul Blair to bring in college kids to enhance the summer program," Turner said. "The older swimmers revealed new possibilities to the kids, motivated the parents, and generally lifted the performance outcome of the whole team. Blair made it happen here in Arkansas."

"I have enormous admiration for Coach Blair as a person—his work ethic, organizational talent, innovative approach to coaching, consistency, and above all professionalism. Nobody in Arkansas swimming ever came close."

Kees Oudegeest

A Swimming Family

Mary Dawn Blair had a demanding role in the Dolphins swimming family. As the coach's wife, she was a tireless cook and gracious hostess for post-practice dinners, holiday parties, and summer boarders, providing a Little Rock home for up to four college girls at a time. She was also a business partner, keeping the Dolphins team finances in order. This was in addition to raising her three daughters, all of whom were Dolphins swimmers.

"The team was part of our family," Mary Dawn said. "I knew most of the families and parents of the swimmers. All the college swimmers would come to our house, and it was pizza and beer every Friday during the summer. The kids that came to train for the Olympics, who were not on our team, also came over for dinner a lot."

With swimmers graduating each year from the team roster, Mary Dawn saw one group influencing another—as one group aged up and qualified for Junior and Senior Nationals, a younger cadre was ready to emulate the success of their older teammates.

"I think his swimmers were so successful because there was always a group stepping up, and the younger swimmers always wanted to be in that group," she said. "Paul made them write down their goals at the beginning of the year. He made them set their minds to believe there were no limits, but you had to work hard. After a

"One of his real gifts was calmness. A quiet confidence is what swimmers need to perform their best at big pressure meets, and a coach has more influence on that than anyone else."

David Guthrie

> "What other mothers have their teenaged son as a captive audience for so many hours a week."
>
> Sonny Hargis

race, he would break it down to his swimmers and make them realize what they needed to do."

Mary Dawn said her husband never thought of his coaching as a job. Seeing people succeed, seeing the fulfillment on the kids' faces was his reward. "I think he felt a sense of accomplishment in helping them reach whatever goals they had," she said.

"He loved it, and he loved his swimmers," she added.

> "Coach Blair never got down or negative. He always thought something great was just around the corner. I attribute my success to that infectious positive attitude. His greatest quality as a coach was making you reach higher."
>
> J. J. Marus

John Hargis, Arkansas' Olympic champion

John Hargis is the first Olympic gold medal swimmer to call Arkansas home. He came from a small town with no public swimming pool. Through his high school years, his parents drove him 90 miles each way to swim practice in Little Rock. And in a field that demands repeated international racing experience, Hargis' first-ever international swim meet was the 1996 Olympic Games at Atlanta.

Hargis began swimming as an eight year old. Three afternoons a week, his mother, Sonny Hargis, drove him from the central Arkansas town of Clinton to the Aqua Kids team practice at the Hendrix College pool in Conway. That drive was an hour each way. The ride increased to an hour and half each way when Hargis turned fourteen and joined the Little Rock Dolphins.

"What other mothers have their teenaged son as a captive audience for so many hours a week," Sonny Hargis said. Though her "captive audience" would unfailingly fall asleep for the rides, Sonny said she never regretted the time dedicated to her son's sport or the quantities of fast food consumed along the way.

"Bob Courtway [Hendrix College Athletic Director and former swim coach] told me that John was really good. He made me promise I wouldn't push him or let anyone burn him out," Sonny Hargis said.

Hargis needed no pushing. He was one of those rare, young persons whose inner drive woke him on time each morning and carried him through school, swim practice, and long periods of travel without complaint. For two summers during his high school years, his parents co-leased a Little Rock apartment with a family from Hot Springs, giving Hargis and Dolphins teammate Lindsey McVey a swimmer's ideal summer. All they had to

1990 Junior Nationals, Mission Viejo, CA. Brian Kindl, Jonathan Kletzel, Manning Field, Basil Hicks, John Hargis, Paul Blair, Priscilla Jones, Lindsey McVey.

do was eat, sleep, and walk to the Racquet Club pool for practice.

Hargis recalled a few "stepping stone" improvements over twelve years of training and racing when he realized his sacrifices and those made by his family were worthwhile.

"One of my first goals was to wear the green Dolphins team parka," he said. "I had to make a Junior National cut to get that."

That goal was accomplished in 1989 when the 14-year old Hargis made his Junior Nationals cut by .03 seconds with a 54.16 in the 100-Yard Backstroke. The green parka motivated him again in 1992, when as a high school senior, he qualified for Senior Nationals. In the 100-Yard Butterfly, Hargis defeated Tom Jager, one of the world's fastest swimmers. Hargis also challenged Jeff Rouse, losing a close backstroke race with the man who would later join him on the US Olympic and US National teams.

"That was a moment when I realized that all the car time and the time not with my buddies had been worth it," Hargis said. "I was at the pinnacle of the sport. That propelled me to college that year."

Hargis swam for Auburn University, where he was a nine-time All-American and Southeast Conference champion in the 100-Yard Butterfly. By 1993, his national stature had been established. When not representing Auburn, Hargis listed the Little Rock Dolphins as his home team, a loyalty to the coach who had brought him so far, whom he said made him "mentally tough enough to compete."

Hargis' swimming prowess peaked in an Olympic year. In March 1996, he was the 1st place qualifier for the US Olympic Team, winning the 100-Meter Butterfly with a lifetime best time of 53.42. He had been seeded 3rd in the event, had never broken 55 seconds, and was rated 25th in the US. His goal had been just to make the finals.

Hargis did not qualify for the 100 Butterfly finals at the Atlanta Olympic Games. But he did win a gold medal as part of the U.S. 400-Meter Medley Relay team.

Hargis today is head swimming coach at Penn State University. The memories of an Olympic season fourteen years ago are still distinct and moving for him, but the

JOHN HARGIS

Hometown: Clinton, Arkansas
Affiliations: USS Club Team, 1989 - 1996
Little Rock Racquet Club
Coach - Paul Blair
University: Auburn University, 1993 - 1996
Coach - David Marsh
Career Highlights: 1993 U S Age Group National Champion
1993 Olympic Festival Gold Medalist
1994-96 NCAA All-American
1996 Olympic Trials Champion: 100m Butterfly

1996 OLYMPIC GOLD MEDALIST

Are Swimmers Smarter Than Other Athletes?

"Swimmers learn on a daily basis to follow the black line, achieve the goal, and work hard to get there. Not many athletes will follow the same line for two hours. You won't find a more structured athlete."

John Hargis

"One of my first goals was to wear the green Dolphins team parka. I had to make a Junior National cut to get that."

John Hargis

1992 Kerr McGee meet. Back: Priscilla Jones, Adam Nelsen, Scott Strauss, John Hargis, Front: Keith McAfee, Lindsey McVey, Ann Hiller, Paul Blair.

Tay Stratton— A Creative Legacy

She's pretty much at home on the pool deck, coming from a family of five swimming sisters. In her competitive years as an age group and college swimmer, she represented Miller Swim Gym, Arkansas Dolphins, and UALR. She's been a professional swimming teacher and coach in Little Rock for more than twenty years.

Tay Stratton has been involved with the best of Arkansas swimming most of her life. She's doing what she loves. Her work rewards her, she said, through the success of her athletes and friendships made.

"I encourage athletes to be creative, to think on their own and take ownership of their training," Stratton said. "When they contribute, I can tailor the training to the personality of the kids."

Creativity is a key element in Stratton's coaching strategies. As she builds team spirit through fun participation, she adapts stroke drills and other techniques to keep the training exciting and effective. The result is an engaging training atmosphere which leads to swimmers' success.

"Tay is one of the most technical coaches I know," UALR coach Amy Gruber Burgess said. "She loves the sport and is dedicated to keeping up with everything."

Stratton started teaching swim lessons in 1989 at the Little Rock Athletic Club. She soon became Aquatics Director and started an after-school team with fourteen

racing and times achieved are no longer the prime remembrance.

"My Olympic memories are more of the people and our friendships, and not so much the racing and pool time," Hargis said. "After the swimming was over, we stayed in the Olympic Village with our friends. I was asked to escort President Clinton around. For three hours, I walked around with the President of the United States and talked to him about everyday things."

Hargis' parents were at the Olympic Trials that spring and at the Atlanta Games that followed. Sonny Hargis recalled those experiences and the years of preparation leading up to them.

"It was a big commitment, but we never looked back," she said. "Now I miss the swimming and the meets. I even miss the driving."

> **What is the Difference Between Sprinters and Distance Swimmers?**
> "Distance swimmers are more introverted, and sprinters are Type A, applying their will power at the onset of a race."
> **Anita Harrison Henry**

Tay Stratton

Dolphins and SMU butterfly champion Matt Twillie was on the Laser coaching staff for several years, sharing his passion for the sport with a new group of children. And today, the Team Coordinator is swim parent Elaine Schienvar, whose five daughters swim for the Laser Team. The family offers a poignant reminder of the household in which Tay Stratton was raised.

In 2007, the Laser Swim Team merged with the Little Rock Arkansas Dolphins. The team name and size have changed, but not Stratton's purpose as a coach and teacher.

"One of my main motivating forces is to instill in my swimmers the work ethic and characteristics of a champion," Stratton said. "I want them to know that they can do anything they want and never limit themselves. That is the freedom a true athlete has."

swimmers. The original plan was simply to help kids stay fit while their parents were working out. But many kids wanted to compete, and their parents wanted a program. The new team joined USA Swimming in 1992 and grew quickly.

Over the years, the Laser team has also become part of the continuum of Arkansas swimming. Laser sprinter Neka Mabry attended the University of Georgia and swam for Coach Harvey Humphries, a former Miller Swim Gym member. Former

> **What is the Difference Between Sprinters and Distance Swimmers?**
> "Distance swimmers are jealous of sprinters because they're in and out so quickly and take all the glory."
> *Mike Neuhofel*

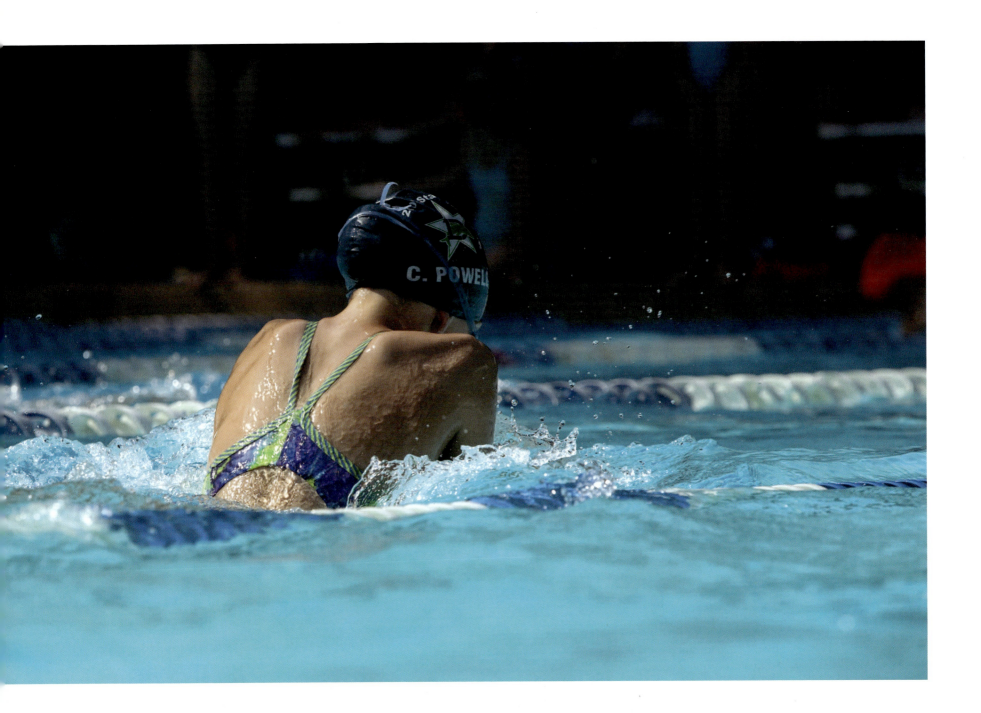

Chapter 9. The Winning Formula: Motivation

A Personal Commitment to Excellence
As young swimmers age up and their skills increase, their incentives for peak performance change. The high-spirited fun of age-group teams often transforms within a few years into a personal commitment to excellence. At each phase of their growth and maturity, champion swimmers cultivate unique aspects of motivation.

"Good swimmers can be born or bred, but great swimmers are born and bred."
— Doug Martin

A gifted few come to the sport with the innate quality often called "a feel for the water," that elusive combination of efficiency and grace. Arkansas' age group prodigies have always had it, from Sue Keith Wrape in the 1940s to Noel Strauss in the 1980s. These natural athletes enter the sport with coordination and skill, a physical capacity rapidly transformed into championship performance.

Others are late bloomers. Years of training and precise coaching are needed to get them onto the winner's platform. International champions Pat Miles and John Hargis peaked as young men. But attentive coaches saw them as age group diamonds in the rough, a gem that would shine only after much polish.

Commitment, Focus, and Goals

"A swimmer is alone four hours a day. He stares at the black line and goes up and down the pool with effort."
— John Hargis

Committed swimmers know hard work yields success. Committed swim families know that swimming is worth the time commitment.

Basil Hicks recalled the shared values of his parents and the Dolphins team. "When I was a kid you had to be really sick to miss practice. The expectation was as a swimmer you don't go home to play video games instead of going to practice. You are at practice, or you are doing homework," Hicks said.

"Water time is important to develop comfort and refine skills, Hicks added, but top kids stay focused during that time."

Being focused involves setting goals and tracking one's progress in achieving them.

> "We pushed each other to be the best we could. We were there to swim faster and reach times that would allow us to compete regionally and nationally."
>
> — Autumn Buddenberg Taylor

But as Mike Neuhofel learned, too much adherence to a goal can be detrimental.

"In 1987, I was the number one seed in the 50 Freestyle at NCAA nationals," Neuhofel said. "I thought I could win if I went 19.5. But Matt Biondi blew me away when he went 19.18 in the heat before me. My goal was my limitation."

As an age group swimmer, Noel Strauss' ultimate goal was to qualify for the U.S. Olympic Team. But as a National Age Group Champion, he studied the Top 16 charts in *Swimming World* Magazine to "find out where I stacked up against other kids in the nation."

"I was lucky to have a group of guys older than me that were very good, working hard in the weight room and going to Junior and Senior Nationals," Strauss said. "I pushed myself to compete against them, rather than the kids in my age group."

Team Pride

Dunking the coach *is part of the Dolphin-Laser team celebration after winning a state championship meet.*

> "I remember swimming with John Hicks and Sean Casey, and they would be yelling encouragements at me in the distance lane. Everybody was focused in the workouts and getting where they needed to be."
>
> — Amy Gruber Burgess

The solitude of training, the "black line" concept, is lost in the emotional intensity of relays and team score announcements. Swimmers affirm themselves through team identity. It is a unique and powerful motivation.

Autumn Buddenberg Taylor recalled the strong friendships of her team at the YWCA and their pride in state champion status. Taylor found a new camaraderie when she joined the Dolphins Team.

"The Racquet Club was a more intense competitive program," Taylor said. "We pushed each other to be the best we could. We were there to swim faster and reach times that would allow us to compete regionally and nationally."

The expectation of success was reflected in the team motto, 'Believe in the Dolphin Difference,' introduced by Paul Blair. Team membership strengthened the swimmers' willingness to work hard in practice and swim fast in races.

"I remember as a kid saying 'This is the Dolphins relay team. We do not lose these relays,'" Basil Hicks said. "We had lots of peer encouragement that made it hard for someone to give up."

Hannah Bakke, a Dolphins age group star who first qualified for the Olympic

Trials when she was 14 years old, confirmed the team belief.

"The Dolphins mind set was that if you lost, it was a mistake," Bakke said. "The expectation was that you would be the best. Coach Blair exuded that confidence. He believed it so much, it made you believe it, too."

For sprinter Mike Neuhofel, the Dolphins team gave him exposure to top level athletes. World class sprinters Steve Crocker and Doug Boyd inspired him to higher achievement. It was exactly what he needed.

"I came out for the team when Tom Genz was on a national level," Neuhofel said. "Without that, I would have been satisfied with Conway High School records and wouldn't have raised my posture higher."

Arkansas high school swimming did not inspire top performance or team identity. Doug Martin said many of his Hall High School fellow students were unaware of a school swimming team.

"Swimming was considered such a minor sport, I was embarrassed to wear my swimming letter jacket to school," Martin said. "The only people that cared were

Men's 200 Free Relay: *(15-18) Broke existing 15-year old LSC record by with a 1:25:50 at the 2010 NSCA Junior National Meet, Orlando, FL. (Left to right) Eric Zheng, Sam Olson, Brooks Wilmoth, Nick McCarthy.*

Dry land exercises *are used throughout the year to build strength, balance, and reflex. Coach Basil Hicks oversees a push-up set on the deck of the LRRC 50-meter pool.*

Teammates and team spirit

Right: Poolside cheers for racing teammates.

Below: Skye Stratton adds some body art to a teammate's back during a quiet moment at a summer swim meet.

other swimmers. People barely knew swimming existed; it was totally obscure."

Despite a natural ability in football and track, Martin found a distinction in swimming that kept him involved.

"It made me different from the other jocks at school," Martin said. "It was also something I could be competitive in. When you are among the best in a sport, you don't want to give it up."

Team Motivation

"Every time you went to the swim meet, it was an instant play date."
Matt Twillie

Team friendships and fun become the first motivation for new swimmers. These are often 10 & Under age groups, but many college coaches will tell you of how well this motivation works for them.

Jan Diner Hildebrandt remembered bunking parties at the YWCA in the 1960s and her coaches, Mary Lou Jaworski and Mickey Burris entertaining the team on bus trips. Rick Witherspoon recalled overnight sessions at the Racquet Club for 24-hour swim-a-thon fundraisers. Susan Letzig Roehrenbeck brought up memories of swim meets at Hendrix College, her friends on floor blankets around her, the college pool giving the meet a special quality.

And there were Laser team trips to regional meets, accompanied by side visits to Sea World and local beaches. Dolphins winter trips included skiing time.

The environment created for the young swimmers gave them a sense of identity and belonging. They experienced feelings of loyalty. They responded by working hard in practice and swimming fast. Parents appreciated the swimming environment and trusted the place where their children were spending time.

"It was fun to go to workouts in the summer and then hang out at the Racquet Club all day, every single day of the summer," Noel Strauss said. "We were there playing together all day. Parents were able to leave us and not worry."

Coach Motivation

"Miller had the love for the kids. You wanted to swim for him."
Sammy Turner

Coaches are surrogate parents. They teach children to build character. They prepare a child for new experiences. When

What is the Difference Between Sprinters and Distance Swimmers?
"There is less difference today when you see how fast swimmers go out in the distance events. We train fast twitch now, even for the mile."
Harvey Humphries

coaches are good motivators, swimmers want to win their approval.

Mary Lou Jaworski experienced this with her team at the YWCA. In 1968, the team's fastest 8 & Under swimmer Keena Rothhammer moved to Texas. Jaworski wasn't convinced the remaining team was strong enough to win the upcoming meet.

"Jan Diner told me I didn't have to worry. She said they would win it for me," Jaworski said

When her YWCA team won the meet by twenty points, Jaworski realized the girls had been letting Keena do the work. She saw that Jan, given the opportunity to respond directly to her coach, would meet the adult expectations placed on her.

Sara Kay Humphries was fourteen years old and the smallest swimmer on the Boys Club team attending the 1949 AAU Junior Olympics at the Shamrock Hotel in Dallas. The 50-meter pool there was the first Humphries had seen. She remembered Jimmy Miller's inspirational pep talk.

"He told me the whole relay depended on me getting a lead in the backstroke first leg," Humphries said. "I swam and got the lead, then passed out in the water. Miller had to jump in and pull me out. The race continued, we got fourth, and I woke up on a stretcher."

John Hargis remembers an experience with Paul Blair at the Indiana University natatorium. When the two of them entered the building, they read the names of numerous Olympic athletes from IU displayed on the walls. Blair told Hargis to visualize his own name on those walls and to focus on what that wall meant to US swimming.

"It was Coach Blair's way of expressing confidence in me," Hargis said. "You wanted to do everything you could to succeed for the man."

Right: "Birthday swims" are a Dolphin-Laser team tradition, with the chosen swimmer racing through a choppy gauntlet of his teammates' splashes.

Below: "Eyes and goggles"

Personal Motivation

"My passion—I love to stand up on the blocks and see who's got what that day."
Larry Golden

The highest motivation comes from within. The swimmer is deeply involved, Dolphin-Laser Head Coach Matt Adams said, because he loves racing and how swimming fast makes him feel.

Harvey Humphries said champion swimmers can be identified by their self motivation and willingness to test themselves. As an example, he suggested how swimmers might react at an outdoor meet canceled by stormy weather.

"Seven kids will cheer that they got out. But one will put his head down and cry," Humphries said. "That one will be the champion."

Many times, talented kids only want to get the race over, Humphries added, but champions want to know what comes next, even in practice. For these athletes, their sport is their passion.

Coaches who understand that passion will challenge their athletes through a demanding training program. Maintaining high quality workouts becomes a test of the athlete's character and partnership with the coach. In this way, a coach challenges their commitment to be the person they pledged to be.

J.J. Marus had this experience with Paul Blair in 1999. Marus was a college graduate who trained with the Dolphins team with the hopes of making a US National Team. Marus said he was inspired by the coaching and the team program in Little Rock, as if he and Blair were on a personal mission to fulfill his goals.

J. J. Marus

> *"Seven kids will cheer that they got out. But one will put his head down and cry. That one will be the champion."*
>
> Harvey Humphries

> **Are Swimmers Smarter Than Other Athletes?**
> "Swimming is going to teach you life lessons at a young age: how to learn from failure, how to go on and be yourself in the end. Swimming makes you a confident person. I think the majority of people that get into swimming, it changes their life."
> **Matt Twillie**

"One time, I missed a few practices when a friend was visiting. Coach Blair was not a guy who cracked the whip, not a domineering figure. But he let me have it. He put me in my place. He had an ability to be forceful and strong yet with no negative response or anger. He knew when to use force and when to be positive and nurturing. I went back to training, determined to prove to him I was still on pace, still willing to do what we had set out to do."
J. J. Marus

> **What is the Difference Between Sprinters and Distance Swimmers?**
> "The distance swimmer's mindset has to be very driven. Sprinters are the kind of people that just want do things as fast as they can. Sprinters are more on the competitive side. They are wired with those fast twitch muscles."
> **Amy Gruber Burgess**

Chapter 10. 2000s

Teams in Transition
Competitive swimming in Central Arkansas changed dramatically in recent years. The decade was marked by a new group of nationally ranked athletes, the tragic loss of Arkansas' most successful coach, and the realignment of Little Rock swim teams, pools, and sponsors. Former swimmers assumed new positions of leadership, and the core values of the sport were renewed with fresh energy and growth.

The decade opened with an Olympic year and the 2000 summer games scheduled at Sydney, Australia. That summer in Little Rock, nine swimmers had qualified for the US Olympic Trials. Four of them were homegrown talent from the Dolphins and Laser teams. Others came from Arkansas swim programs and out-of-state colleges.

2000 U.S. Olympic Trials Qualifiers
- **Matt Weghorst**, 20, of North Little Rock. A Senior Nationals finalist, he made his Trials cut in three events a year and a half earlier.
- **Hannah Bakke**, 15, of Little Rock. She is a High School All-American and Junior Nationals champion.
- **John Hargis**, 25, of Clinton. He is the defending Olympic Trials champion in the 100-Meter Butterfly and a gold medalist in the 1996 Olympics.
- **Neka Mabry**, 17, of Little Rock. She is a Junior Nationals champion and High Point winner.
- **Bobby O'Bryan**, 18, of Fort Smith. He is a two-time winner at Junior Nationals.
- **John Berry**, 20, of Houston. He is a Division II National Champion from Ouachita Baptist University.
- **Kicker Vencill**, 22, of Franklyn, KY.
- **J. J. Marus**, 24, of Greensboro, NC.
- **Drew Dischinger**, 23, of Kansas City, MO.

In the early years of the decade, the Lasers' Mark Barham was 2nd in the nation in the 200-Meter Butterfly. The only 13-14 age group swimmer in the US faster than Barham was an up-and-comer from Baltimore named Michael Phelps. Other National Age Group Top 16 swimmers from this period included Hannah Bakke, Neka Mabry, and Daniel Pupkowski.

In 2007, the Dolphins and the Lasers teams merged. Age group swimmers on the new Dolphin-Laser Team continued to place in the Top 10 nationally through the decade.

2000 Olympic Trials qualifiers: *Hannah Bakke and Bobby O'Bryan.*

Satellite Teams and Other Changes

In the early 2000s, the Dolphins Team began branching out to new areas of Pulaski County. In Jacksonville, a new community center was built and Blair advised on racing components in the pool's multi-use plan. A satellite swim program was established there, as well as in Sherwood and Cabot. Training was conducted by Keith McAfee, longtime assistant coach and team administrator.

Other changes in the local swim scene followed the 2005 selection of Paul Blair as the women's Associate Head Swim Coach at UALR. (The men's program had been dropped by the university in 1996 as part of its compliance with NCAA equity and Title IX policy.) The Dolphins team now had UALR as its home pool. But by this time, Blair had already begun receiving treatment for prostate cancer. His health was declining.

In 2003, former Dolphins distance champion Basil Hicks, a Yale graduate and a science teacher in the Little Rock School

Neka Mabry *began swimming for the Lasers and Coach Tay Stratton at age ten. Among many accomplishments, she set numerous State and LSC records, was repeatedly ranked in the Top 16 in the Nation, was High Point Winner at Junior Nationals 1997, attended two USS National Select Camp at the Olympic Training Center in Colorado, and qualified for Senior Nationals and the 2000 Olympic Trials.*

She was a member of the University of Georgia's NCAA National Champion Team and an SEC Champion in the 100-Yard Backstroke. Many of her relays set NCAA, American, and US Open records. In her last swim meet as a Lady Bulldog, her relay team set a world record in the 200-Meter (sc) Freestyle Relay.

Dolphin-Laser Top 10 National Age Group Ranking since 2007

Name	Age	Year	Event	National Rank
Jordan Sweet	10	2009	100-Meter Breaststroke	6th
	9	2008	200-Yard Breaststroke	6th
Jessie Garrison	13	2009	800-Meter Freestyle	1st
	13	2009	200-Meter Butterfly	2nd
Delaney Haralson	10	2009	200-Meter Butterfly	9th
	10	2009	1500-Meter Freestyle	4th
Tim Barnett	12	2007	1500-Meter Freestyle	6th
Olivia Keith	9	2010	50-Meter Breaststroke	9th
Ravi Sun	14	2009	200-Meter backstroke	7th
Shelby Burleson	12	2009	1500-Meter Freestyle	10th

  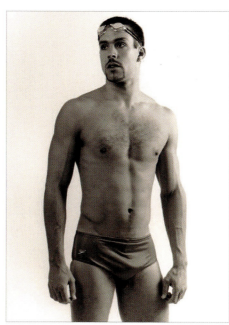

The Boys of Summer, 2000

The Dolphin Team fundraising project was to be a photo calendar featuring the young men training at the Racquet Club. Though the project was not completed, the photos remain a testament to the health and vitality of the athletes.

Top: Kicker Vencill, Matt Weghorst, J. J. Marus.
Bottom: Paul Peavey, John Hargis, Carlos Santander

- Vencill and Weghorst were on a US National team that competed in the 2001 World University Games at Beijing. Blair was a coach on that trip.
- Marus was on the US National Team that competed 1999 Pan Pac Games at Sydney.
- Paul Peavey, 18, was a Junior Nationals and US Open qualifier. He began racing at 6 years old.
- John Hargis was a US National team member for several years after winning a gold medal at the 1996 Olympics.
- Carlos Santander trained with the Dolphins in 2000. A native of Venezuela, he swam in the 1996 and 2000 Olympics.

Photographs by Dixie Knight Photography

Kicker Vencill

Among the top swimmers who came to Little Rock to train with Paul Blair, Kicker Vencill has had the most controversy.

In 2002, Vencill tested positive for banned substances and was suspended from international competition for two years. Vencill fought back, and in 2005, he won a legal judgment against the company that provided him with multivitamins contaminated with steroid precursors.

He was a victim of tainted supplements, but his suspension from swimming was never reduced nor set aside. Though he received a financial settlement, he missed a shot at the 2004 Athens Olympics while the matter was resolved.

Vencill was a US Top 10 100-meter freestyler and a member of the 1999 US National Team that competed in the World University Games in China. He was a student at Western Kentucky State at that time, and his coach, former world record holder Steve Crocker, recommended Vencill spend his summers training with Blair. After three summers in Little Rock, Vencill continued his training in California, where the testing and suspension took place.

Vencill today works as an ocean lifeguard at Venice and Santa Monica. He is planning to begin paramedic training at UCLA. He also does outreach education with the US Anti Doping Agency to raise athletes' awareness of their rights and responsibilities with supplements.

"For a while I was bitter about what I had lost," Vencill said. "But your shelf life in swimming is so short. My obligation now is to give back to the sport. I take pride in that."

District, began assisting Blair with coaching the team. As Blair's illness advanced, the need for a replacement head coach became more apparent. In 2004, Blair asked his most successful swimmer to return to Little Rock and take over the Dolphins team coaching.

"Coach called me on a Sunday, and I was actually in the car on the way to my wedding," John Hargis said. On the coaching staff at Penn State, Hargis was not seeking a job. "But when Paul Blair calls, you don't say no."

Hargis had a season overlap with his former coach before Blair died. Hargis stayed on as Head Coach for the next three years, and then he accepted his current position as Head Coach at Penn State.

Following the 2007 merger of the Dolphins and Laser teams, Tay Stratton continued to lead the age group program at the Racquet Club. Matt Adams, a product of northwest Arkansas swimming programs and a recent University of Missouri at Rolla graduate, was hired to coach the senior swimmers. Basil Hicks

> **What is the Difference Between Sprinters and Distance Swimmers?**
> "A sprinter is geared for speed. Distance swimmers may love to do that but don't have fast twitch muscles. So they get stuck in what might be seen as a boring event."
> **Steve Crocker**

became the Dolphin-Laser Assistant Coach. The senior team trains at UALR in the winter. In the summer, senior and developmental teams work out at the LRRC 50-meter pool.

Numerous Dolphins and Laser swimmers have taken leadership roles in the swimming community in central Arkansas. At UALR, Amy Gruber Burgess is the Head Swim Coach and Tom Genz is the Aquatics Coordinator for the 50-meter pool in the student center.

Similar to her four sisters, Tasha Stratton followed her competitive years with swim coaching and teaching. She continues today as coach of the Masters swimmers training at the Racquet Club. And for several years, Matt Twillie was the Assistant Coach for the Lasers.

Two former swimmers, both competitors in the 1990s, are actively working with a new generation of age group athletes. Patrick Bass is now head coach of the new Central Arkansas Swim Club. Eimear Ryan is the Aquatics Director at the Little Rock Athletic Club, where the earliest swim lessons and development classes continue to be offered.

Still the team to beat

With their fifth consecutive win at the ASI State Championships in 2010, the Dolphin-Laser Team is retaining its decades-old status as "the team to beat." The team won short course and long

Paul Blair: A Positive Attitude

Paul Blair with High Point winners Shannon Murphy and Landon Meeks at the 2004 State Age Group Championships.

Paul Blair died in 2006 at the age of 57. He had been battling prostate cancer for several years. Until the illness overcame him, Blair remained active in his coaching and his healthy lifestyle. His positive attitude never faltered, even when he was in a wheelchair on the pool deck.

David Guthrie recalled his last encounter with Blair at a national Masters Swimming meet in Florida, "Paul was still on deck, inspiring everyone," Guthrie said. "His grace awed me. I was thankful to be around him and learn from him in those last days."

SELF PORTRAIT
Paul Blair

- **DATE AND PLACE OF BIRTH** May 19, 1949, Dover Ohio.
- **MY FAVORITE KIND OF DAY BEGINS WITH** Getting ready for a morning practice, going for a long run four mornings a week and doing weights another two.
- **MY HEROES INCLUDE** My grandfather; Tom Patton, who was my coach at the YMCA; Tom Grall, who was my college coach; and Sam Freas, who recently was the president of the International Swimming Hall of Fame.
- **WHEN TALENTED KIDS DON'T WANT TO WORK HARD, A GREAT COACH** Will allow them to understand that talent will only take them so far. You can only be as good as you want to be.
- **EVERY GREAT SWIMMER** Has to understand that along with winning is defeat. You learn more from your disappointments than you do your glory.
- **COMPETITION** Is a wonderful thing. Competition can teach you so much about yourself, what it takes to be successful and ultimately, to be good.
- **COACHING HAS TAUGHT ME** It's up to you to decide how strong you are and what level of success you want to have and if adversity is going to slow you down or motivate you to be better.
- **POKER HAS TAUGHT ME** That no matter what you do in life, in order to be the best at what you do, you have to be the smartest.
- **I'M GRATEFUL** for the Pat Rileys, for Chris Peterson and Richard Turner at the University of Arkansas at Little Rock and for the Country Club of Little Rock—they are wonderful people.
- **I WANT THE WORLD TO KNOW** How proud I am of our three daughters and how much I love my wife.
- **WORDS TO SUM ME UP** If you get knocked down, stand up and do it again. Stand up and do it again.

Self Portrait
Arkansas Gazette, *September 4, 2005*

Found among writings in Paul Blair's office
"The longer I live, the more I realize the impact of attitude on life. We have a choice every day regarding the attitude we will embrace for that day. We cannot change our past. We cannot change the inevitable. The only thing we can do is play on the one string we have, and that is our attitude...I am convinced that life is 10% what happens to me and 90% how I react to it. And so it is with you...we are in charge of our attitudes."

"Paul was still on deck, inspiring everyone. His grace awed me. I was thankful to be around him and learn from him in those last days."

— David Guthrie

On the Deck with the Lasers, 2000: *Eimear Ryan, Coach Matt Twillie, and Aaron Cox*

The Arkansas Dolphin-Laser Swim Team has been named a 2010 USA Swimming Bronze Medal Club *as one of the Top 200 clubs in the country.*

course state champion meets in all divisions, and seven swimmers qualified to attend Junior Nationals.

The team has a balance of top achievers and eager 8 & Under record setters. Three swimmers were ranked in National Top 16, and 13-year-old Jessie Garrison, who learned to swim in a Dolphins' summer league program, was ranked 1st in the nation in the 800-Meter Freestyle and 2nd in the 200 Butterfly.

The newest record-setter in the age group program is eight-year old Ryland Sun, who broke two of Arkansas' oldest swimming records at the Trey Heye Memorial Invitational held at UALR.

Long-standing State and LSC records were also surpassed by the Dolphin-Laser team in 15-18 men's relays at the 2010 Junior Nationals Championship. In the 200-Yard Medley Relay, a 27-year old record was broken (1:52.19—Sam Olson, Troy Esentan, Eric Zheng, Brooks Wilmoth). In the 200-Yard Freestyle Relay, a 15-year old record was surpassed. (1:25.50—Zheng, Wilmouth, Nick McCarthy, Sam Olson). [LSC/Local Swimming Committee is a regional grouping of swim programs by US Swimming].

Other top Dolphin-Laser swimmers, all record breakers in 2010, include Shelby Cox, Troy Esentan, Jordan Sweet, and Arianna Shojahee.

The future of Arkansas swimming

"I think given the number of participants in the state, the individual success rate has been very high. Nothing says that better than the number of national champions produced."

— Trip Strauss

Matt Adams recognizes the heritage of the Dolphins team is his to carry on. He also knows that swimmers today need a different coaching environment than in the past. The techniques used by Jimmy Miller in the 1960s, including corporal punishment, would send age grouper swimmers running for the locker rooms. And the quiet, motivational techniques used by Paul Blair would be successful with a shrinking number of athletes.

The issue is getting kids ready to do the training, Adams believes.

"To develop into a top-level athlete is to learn what it takes to train," Adams said. "Many swimmers today have a hard time grasping that."

Are Swimmers Smarter Than Other Athletes?
"I solved a lot of calculus and computer problems while in the water."
— **Anita Heil Parisi**
Hall High School valedictorian 1982

Dolphin-Laser Swimmers Rank "TOP 10" In the Nation, 2009-2010

The National Age Group Award from United States Swimming is given to United States swimmers that have ranked "Top 10" in the nation in their gender and age bracket. United States Swimming has nearly 300,000 competitive athletes.

Jessie Garrison (above left) ranked number one in the 13-14 year old girls 800-Meter Freestyle, 9:06.74. She also received "Top 10" ranking in four other events; second in the 200-Meter Butterfly, seventh in the 200-Yard Butterfly, seventh in the 400-Meter Freestyle and eighth in the 11-12 girls in the 1650-Yard Freestyle.

Ravi Sun (above center) ranked number seven in the Nation in the 13-14 boys 200-Meter Backstroke, 2:17.39.

Shelby Burleson (above right) ranked tenth in the 11-12 girls 1500-Meter Freestyle, 18:29.30.

As a result of their performances, the swimmers attended the United States Swimming Select Camps. These camps invite some of the top athletes in the nation for training, building peer relations, and improving their understanding of the process of becoming an Olympic champion.

New Kids on Deck

The Central Arkansas Swim Club "Racers" (see logo below) made their first appearance in 2008. The team was started by North Little Rock native Patrick Bass and Onat Tungac, both All-American swimmers at Henderson State University. The team trains at the North Little Rock Boys Club, has a satellite swimming program at El Dorado, and is planning a second program at Bryant. Bass, chosen as ASI Coach of the Year in 2010, said his swimmers have already broken fourteen state records. CASC swimmer Lee Smothers was 8th in the nation with a 28.57 in the 50-Meter Butterfly, 11-12 age group, in 2010.

"Arkansas swimming has been part of my life forever," Bass said. "I found my love in coaching. I'm excited to keep giving back."

> "For Arkansas to produce and maintain swimming at the level we saw in the 80s and 90s, we need to transition the kids from summer league and high school swimming to the club experience. We need to have pools at our public schools like other states."
>
> Richard Turner

The choices today for youth sports are extensive. A swim coach competes with soccer, gymnastics, and other sports finding a niche among the 10 & Under crowd. Perhaps more significantly, Adams is challenged by the short attention span of many of today's adolescents.

"In training today, the majority of kids need you to break it up more, make it more engaging in smaller, shorter groupings," Adams said.

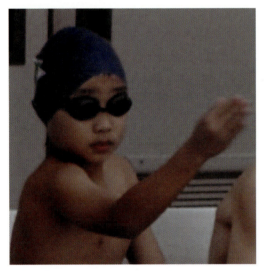

Ryland Sun is the newest record-setter in the eight-year old age group. In 2010, Ryland broke two of Arkansas' oldest swimming records at the Trey Heye Memorial Invitational held at UALR.

8 & Under	New Record	Old Record
25-Yard Freestyle	13.70	14.4*
25-Yard Backstroke	16.95	17.0**

* 1967 Ricky Witherspoon
** 1975 Jim Bryan

Similarly, Arkansas swimming has to become more engaging to gain a larger share of public attention and reach larger numbers of youth. Summer league programs are fulfilling for most families, and parent involvement is critical for that success. But most children don't advance to year-round club programs.

"For Arkansas to produce and maintain swimming at the level we saw in the 80s and 90s, we need to transition the kids from summer league and high school swimming to the club experience," Richard Turner said. "We need to have pools at our public schools like other states."

Arkansas swimming is growing, Tom Genz believes, but public schools can't provide the facilities or the support. A high school or junior high with its own pool and swim team, with a peer group of swimmers at the school, with pep rallies at school before a meet—this scenario, common in many other states, is not a realistic possibility in Arkansas in the foreseeable future, Genz said.

Swimming will grow in Arkansas when people are inspired, Rick Witherspoon said. A Dolphins swimmer in the 1970s, Witherspoon saw his coaches inspire the founding board members and parents.

"Swimming met with success and acceptance by proving it was a great sport and a great character builder for kids, that it can bring so much to one's life," Witherspoon said.

Other observers of the sport believe the efficiency of hydro dynamics, as racers learn to maximize the advantages of underwater power, will draw media attention and boost the popular appeal of swimming.

In USA Swimming clubs across Arkansas today, young swimmers are being taught the latest streamline body position, arms fully extended, torso whipping out a graceful and powerful dolphin kick for the underwater push off. The technique is a far cry from the sport's early years when little or no attention was given to how one pushed off the wall.

They may become Olympic champions or age group record breakers. Or they might simply be team members who give their best. And for that achievement alone, we will want to stand up and cheer.

Redesigned team logo *following the 2007 merger of the Lasers and the Dolphins.*

Are Swimmers Smarter Than Other Athletes?

"Definitely not. It takes some measure of insanity to wake in the morning and jump in cold water. Swimmers lose a little intelligence there."

Neka Mabry

Chapter 11. To An Athlete Dying Young

In Loving Memory of Dolphin-Laser Swimmers

Aaron Cox

Aaron Cox
December 7, 1982–May 5, 2009

Captain Aaron David Cox was an open-hearted and enthusiastic member of the Central High School and Laser Swim Teams. After graduating from the United States Naval Academy in 2005, he enlisted in the United States Marine Corps. Aaron died during a training flight when his Super Cobra helicopter crashed near San Diego County. His personal decorations included the Global War on Terrorism Medal and the National Defense Service Medal. He is remembered for the kindness and loyalty he consistently gave freely to his family, friends and country, and for a wisdom beyond his years.

Trey Heye
November 9, 1993–December 6, 2000

Trey Heye was an animated member of the Dolphins Swim Team from 1998 to 2000. A little boy full of aspirations, at age 5 he was one of the youngest and smallest swimmers on the team. Trey died in the hospital due to a series of medical errors involving medication and an allergic reaction during the Holiday Invitational swim meet. It was renamed the Trey Heye Memorial Meet in his memory. Trey left a legacy of love for this sport to his brothers; with an amazing intelligence, a compassionate and loving heart, and a talent for swimming, he was loved by all those who knew him.

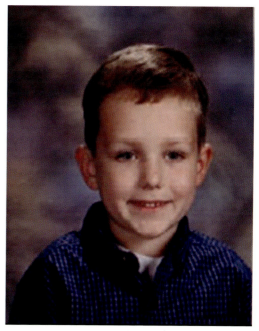

Trey Heye

"Some swimmers, like Aaron Cox, had incredible leadership skills. Others had discipline. And others just tried and tried and gave us determination. Both Mary Grace and Aaron offered so much. Every child contributes in some way and is important to a team."

Tay Stratton

Mary Grace Tucker

Mary Grace Tucker
May 5, 1994–July 31, 2005

Mary Grace Tucker was a spirited and ambitious member of the Laser Swim Team and a motivated individual who was adored by her teammates. Mary Grace died in a car accident on the way home from the 2005 Long Course State Meet in Bentonville, Arkansas. Loved and cherished by her teammates, they honored her memory by renaming the Laser Summer "Red Hot" Swim meet to the Mary Grace Tucker Memorial Invitational.

Gary Schultz
December 30, 1961–March 18, 1978

Gary Schultz was a bright, energetic, young man who swam for the Miller Swim Gym and the Dolphins Swim Team. His teammates described him as "larger than life." A strong competitor, Gary excelled in distance swimming, namely the mile. His aspirations for swimming were cut short before his senior year, when he passed away due to a cardiac arrhythmia. Arkansas Swimming, Inc. honored him with the Gary Schultz Memorial trophy, an annual award to Arkansas' overall top swimmer.

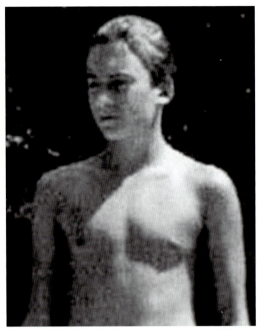
Gary Schultz

Chapter 12. Arkansas Masters Swimming

A Lifetime of Fitness and Competition

The phenomenon of adult swimming and racing proves that one is never too old to enjoy the thrills of competition and the benefits of fitness. In Arkansas, a number of former competitors have returned to the water. Like their younger counterparts, some have become national champions.

"Age, Cunning, Deceit and Treachery Can Defeat Youth and Skill."
Arkansas Masters Swim Club motto

Masters swimming can be described as a competitive program for those too stubborn to quit. While many members of the state-wide Arkansas Masters Swim Club swim for fitness or recreation, the state's adult racers share a particular tenacity. They are defiantly unwilling to give up the pre-race adrenalin rush and surge of vitality that swimmers of every age experience.

Despite the club's motto, adult racers do not have to outwit or compete against young athletes. The program has five-year age brackets that keep the competitive field in balance. In contrast to age-group swimming, Masters swimming "aging up" means gaining the advantage as the youngest racer in your age group. The Arkansas club, incorporated as a nonprofit organization in 1975, is one of more than 1,000 adult swim programs across the country. Arkansas' 145 registered Masters swimmers are among the 50,000 members of the national organization, US Masters Swimming.

The First Masters Meet

The first Arkansas Masters swimming meet was held in 1972 at the Thrasher Boys Club. Participants included prominent names in Arkansas adult swimming at the time—Jimmy Miller, Mary Oudegeest, John Brooks, Benny Wise, and Mary Lou Jaworski.

Masters swimming was nothing new to Mary Oudegeest, the former world record holder in multiple events and professional distance swimmer. She had swum only a month earlier at the 1972 US Masters National Short Course Championships in San Mateo, California. At that meet, Mary won six of her seven events and set national records for the Women's 30-34 age group in the 1,650 (22:08.74), the 500 (6:27.10), and the 200 Yard Freestyle (2:27.30).

Of that original Arkansas Masters group, only former diving champion Benny Wise was still testing his swimming skills in 2008 when, for the second time, he completed the 1.5 mile Alcatraz Sharkfest Swim in San Francisco Bay's 60-degree water. Wise was accompanied in the 2008 event by Arkansas Masters swimmer Ron Bank.

A New York native and a competitive swimmer in his younger years, Bank moved to Arkansas in 1981. He was joined by former swimmers Jaworski, Charlie Matthews, and Rick Field in revitalizing the Masters program. The club organized Masters swim meets with the help of local swim coaches and pools. In the 1980s and 1990s, Masters meets were held at the

> "We promised to make the Marquis de Sade Swim Meet hard enough so that you had to be at least mildly disturbed and nearly seriously demented to swim it."
>
> Ron Bank

Little Rock Racquet Club, YMCA, and YWCA. Lake swims were conducted at Lakewood in North Little Rock and Lake Norrell in Saline County.

A Social Network for Swimmers

Unlike Florida, California and other states with numerous Masters swim clubs, Arkansas' single club became a social network for swimmers from across the state who trained separately. Ida Hlavacek from Mountain Home and Bud Jackson and Barnett Phillips from Fort Smith organized several meets. Masters swimmers from border states Oklahoma, Texas, and Missouri frequently attended.

Never at a loss for fun or creativity, the Arkansas club created specialty events, such as the Hendrix Pentathlon, which featured individual medley races, and the "Marquis de Sade Swim Meet," where participants had to complete a 200 Butterfly, a 400 IM and a 1650 Freestyle. Little Rock advertising executive Jim Johnson had created a Marquis de Sade logo for a local runners club, and he granted use of a modified design for the swim meet.

"We promised to make the Marquis de Sade Swim Meet hard enough so that you had to be at least mildly disturbed and nearly seriously demented to swim it," Bank said.

Arkansas Masters Swim Club members Ron and Kay Bank brought the state banner to the 1983 Masters National Championships at Fort Lauderdale. Bank was the driving force behind the club's annual lake swims, one-mile swims, and Marquis de Sade events for many years.

In the 1980s, Arkansas Masters swimmers began attending U.S. Masters National Championships, and many of them have been repeat winners in their age groups. Arkansas Masters swimmers with multiple national championship wins include David Gillanders, a Bronze Medalist in the 200-Meter Butterfly at the 1960 Olympics; distance freestyler and

> **What is the Difference Between Sprinters and Distance Swimmers?**
> "After fifty yards in any race, we have established who the faster swimmer is. Anything further than fifty yards is superfluous."
>
> **Ron Bank**

backstroker Marvin Schwartz; sprinters Doug Martin and Larry Golden; backstroker Frank Lorge; and Bud Jackson, the Fort Smith phenomenon who now competes in the 90-94 age group.

"The stories I enjoy the most are of older people still trying to achieve faster times," Bank said. "Del Schmand, at age 69, swam a 1500 meter race and made the comment he could do better. At the age of 70, he set a national record in the event."

The Arkansas club, as well as US Masters Swimming, maintain detailed databases to track performance. Accurate record keeping is essential for adult racers who, like fishermen, may tend to enlarge their achievements. "The older we get, the faster we were" is a familiar Masters' swimming motto.

World Record-Breaking Relay, 2nd Place Finish

A Dolphin Masters team broke a world record in the 200-Meter Medley Relay (160+ age group) at the US Masters Long Course National Championships, Woodlands, Texas, August, 1990. Their time of 1:59.71 finished in second place. Relay swimmers were Frank Lorge (front left), Rick Field (front right), Doug Martin (back left), and John Stein (back right).

Arkansas swimmers won two events in the 40-44 age group at the meet. Lorge won the 200-Meter Backstroke in 2:27.87, and Marvin Schwartz (front center) won the 800-Meter Freestyle in 9:54.12. The victories were the first national titles for each swimmer.

Field and Martin had previous Masters national titles. In 1987, Field won the 100-Meter Breaststroke in 1:18.92 (45-49 age group). And at the 1988 Masters Short Course National Championships, Doug Martin won the 50-Yard Freestyle in 21.30 (35-39 age group), setting a new American record.

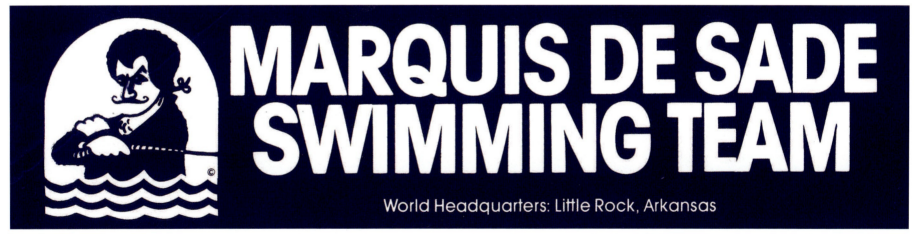

Membership in the Marquis de Sade group *was gained after a one-day competition where Masters Swimmers completed a 400 IM, a 200 Butterfly, and 1,650 Freestyle. The team logo was originally designed by Little Rock advertising executive Jim Johnson for his running club. Johnson added the waves and donated the logo with the hope the event would attract only the "seriously deranged" athlete.*

"I see fit older athletes at Masters Nationals. Their options in life are still open. That's my goal in life."

David Guthrie

Racing with Age Group Swimmers

Over the years, Arkansas Masters swimmers have trained alongside age group teams and competed in age group meets as preparation for their Masters racing. Benefitting from new coaching techniques and their own commitment to the sport, some masters swimmers have achieved lifetime bests, swimming faster in their 40s than they did when in high school or college. A recent example is Little Rock's Brad Eichler, who, at 43 years old, swam the 100-Meter Butterfly in 1:00.62 and won 2nd place at the 2009 Masters Long Course Nationals.

In response to the increasing demand of its adult athletes, the Little Rock Racquet Club, as well as clubs in northwest Arkansas, currently offers coached Masters workouts. A large number of triathletes attend those sessions.

A Lifetime Pursuit

David Guthrie is the most accomplished Masters' swimmer with Arkansas ties. A Hendrix College graduate, Guthrie, 50, is on the faculty of the architecture school at Rice University. He is a former Little Rock Dolphins swimmer and holder of numerous Masters national and world records in breaststroke. He sees Masters swimming as a lifetime pursuit whose benefits include health, vitality, and new creative challenges.

"Swimming is a lifestyle that opens your mind in such a positive way. I'm constantly learning to keep it fresh, to explore something new," Guthrie said. "I see fit older athletes at Masters Nationals. Their options in life are still open. That's my goal in life."

Guthrie believes new Masters records will continue to be set, that people will continue to improve with age and redefine what is possible. With its sequence of age groups, Masters swimming allows people to achieve lifetime bests and still get better, he said. The real value, however, is not shown on a stopwatch.

"If you're disappointed with a particular swim, you need to zoom out a little bit and remember that challenging yourself is in itself a victory," Guthrie said. "Swimming fast or slow is far less important than a willingness to test yourself."

No Kidding Around
Going Stroke for Stroke with Young Swimmers
by Marvin Schwartz
SWIM Magazine, September 1996

The 12-year-old boy walked over from the next lane and stood before me, the top of his head reaching to just below my chin. He looked up at me with the meanest sneer he could muster.

"Marvin," he said, poking a finger in my chest, "you're going down today."

We raced a 200 free that morning, and when it was over, my young teammate had come close but had not been able to beat me. Yet I knew it was just a matter of days, that he would soon drop seconds from his time while I struggled to hold steady. And later that summer, he did just that. He had his rite of passage, and I began, once again, the search for a new rabbit from the promising age group swimmers on our team.

As a Masters swimmer training and competing with a strong age group team, I am used to the exhilaration and humiliation of racing kids young enough to be my grandchildren. Though not for all, the experience has clear advantages. Being part of the team and having a coach who runs daily structured workouts compensates for living in an area where there are no Masters teams that train on my desired level. Nor are there enough nearby Masters meets to provide the racing opportunities I need.

Our coach, Paul Blair of the Arkansas Dolphins Little Rock Racquet Club swim team, tells us that to swim fast we need repeated opportunities to race. So, each year I renew my United States Swimming membership and continue the curious phenomenon of age group training for Masters swimmers.

Technical Benefits

Constant exposure to new and effective techniques is the primary benefit of swimming with a USA Swimming club. Like other Masters swimmers, I have read articles on stroke mechanics and body position in SWIM. But when I got in the water, the same old habits emerged and the same mistakes were repeated. Today, I find the best way to learn the tight tuck of a flip turn or the streamline push-off technique is simply to take an underwater view of my 16-year old teammates as they come shooting off the wall with their arms fully extended, their hips rolling, and their legs whipping out a dolphin kick that propels them nearly half the pool length.

And, I've replaced my old flat-footed swing-arm racing dive with a more efficient track position on the blocks by carefully watching how my young associates do it.

Swimming with age groupers, I've also learned how to structure workouts across the complete season. Blair's training focuses on peak performance at the end of season championship meet, which follows a progression over several months through aerobic, endurance, pace and speed work. Age group swimmers on

Mixed Age Groups: Masters swimmers (standing in water from left) Keith Dixon, Trip Strauss, and Marvin Schwartz with some of their young teammates and Coach Paul Blair of the Little Rock Racquet Club Swim Team.

the Dolphin team repeat these cycles two or three times every year. They target key meets and build their training schedules around them. Masters competitive seasons peak at short and long course nationals, which usually follow soon after a USA Swimming junior or senior national championship meet. With our training pattern so well matched, it's easy to adapt the Masters swimmer's training needs to the age group cycles.

Age group training offers a serious challenge, however. Training twice a day at up to 8,000 yards per workout is not feasible for a person who must work for a living. And the intensity of age group training and racing requires significant rest time. Older swimmers need longer recuperation time following peak exertion. This is most obvious at age group meets where four or five races per half-day session are the norm for each swimmer. As much as we'd like to, few Masters swimmers can perform at that level.

Extreme Enthusiasm

The enthusiasm of training with a young team tends to push one to extremes. The result is a tendency to over-train, particularly during midseason cycles when high yardage workouts are most common. The result can be a residual fatigue that lingers through the season until the championship taper begins.

The enthusiasm of training with a young team tends to push one to extremes. The result is a tendency to over-train, particularly during midseason cycles when high yardage workouts are most common.

> "I told him 'you're 17 and you've just been beaten by a 45-year-old man. How does that make you feel?'"

The lesson here is that midseason competitions must be accepted as part of the training program. At this phase of the season, the race experience is more important than the final time. My real challenge will come at the season championships. This is tough to accept when the young swimmers are dropping times at each meet.

Many Masters swimmers may view their time in the water as a chance to get away from their kids. Yet the teenagers on my team are the best I've ever met. I might feel that way only because I don't have to live with them. But there's no denying that a genuine camaraderie and a sense of team spirit develops. I'm glad when they drop times and go fast, but I want to go fast, too. I don't think I'll drop eight or ten seconds each season, though.

Survival Factor

So, humility becomes a clear survival factor. It's a lesson I learned when a coach once approached me after a race and thanked me profusely for beating his star swimmer who had just loafed through a 100 meter butterfly. Said the coach, "I told him 'you're 17 and you've just been beaten by a 45-year-old man. How does that make you feel?'" The coach didn't ask how it made me feel to hear his logic, but he had a team to motivate and I was convenient for doing so at the moment.

These moments are compensated for by the encouragement and admiration Masters swimmers can receive at age group meets. Swim parents gaze with envy, and officials cheer and offer encouragement. The "old man" is the crowd's sentimental favorite. But the status carries with it a high performance burden. Age groups swim meets and age group training are high-intensity physical challenges. The parents might be impressed, but to their fast kids, I'm just another body to be passed on the way to the finish line.

A father once approached me at a swim meet and asked my lane assignment for an upcoming heat. "My son is in the lane next over," the guy said. "Kick his butt." I wanted to tell the man that I viewed his son as a fellow competitor and that I had nothing but admiration for the boy. The truth was clearly shown in the heat sheets, however. The boy's entry time was far ahead of mine. And the race quickly confirmed how unable I was to kick his butt or anyone else's in that age group. It's tough being a role model these days.

I once joined the George Washington University swim team for a workout, coached by my old Syracuse University teammate and great Masters swimmer John Flannigan. I emerged from the 7,200-yard work out with numerous scrapes on my legs and sides, having been repeatedly swept into the lane ropes as 20-year-old bodies charged past me. Moments such as these quickly reinforce the reality that it is not easy to keep up.

A Sense of Humor

Age group training must be approached with a sense of humor. When a kick set gets beyond my range, I put on my fins and laugh when the kids cry "no fair." When a repeat set leaves me hugging the wall for breath, I try skipping every other interval and finishing the set at an aerobic level, then just grin as my young teammates rant and rave.

A good age group coach will recognize a Masters' contribution to the team. Just as swimmers can set a good example for their younger peers, so a Masters swimmers' presence can add stability and focus to a team workout. Sometimes, kids can get absolutely goofy in practice. A Masters swimmer can help a group keep on time and on count through a long set. On the other hand, a bunch of giggly kids can reveal the lighter side of the rigorous workout.

Masters swimming teaches us that we can never be too old to compete or enjoy this vital activity. Age group training is a way to do this in high spirits. Blair constantly reminds his swimmers to set personal goals, and, in turn, I am reminded of what my goals as a Masters number should be. Achieving them, however, does not always coincide with the desires of my young teammates.

My 12-year-old son, for example, is a member of the Dolphins team, and we work out together and travel to meets together. It's a pleasure to be part of his growth and to watch him overcome new challenges.

I'm just not looking forward to the day when I hear him express his goals in those prophetic words, "Dad, you're going down today!"

Chapter 13. The Winning Formula: Life Impact

A Lasting Commitment of Values
The lessons learned and the habits gained from swimming shape lives and careers. Many former Arkansas swimmers demonstrate the same positive commitment to their families, communities, and their professions as they did in their competitive years. Those values last long after the last lap is swum.

> *"When you commit yourself to becoming a serious swimmer, it pretty much dominates your life. You are training all the time."*
> — Trip Strauss

Former Dolphins swimmer Trip Strauss described his age group swim training as "harder than anything else I've ever done in my life," adding, "What I tell kids today is if you can do that, nothing in your life will be harder."

A successful money manager, Strauss today reflects the professional characteristics of many former swimmers, a large number of whom have become financial analysts, teachers, coaches, medical professionals, and sales representatives. As a group, swimmers interviewed for this history have been drawn toward careers that rely on independent thinking and analytical skills. They tend to be self motivated problem-solvers.

Swimmers who took their sport to heart carry their learned skills into their adult lives. Hannah Bakke is a good example. As a 26-year old, the former All-American swimmer is completing a Masters Degree in Counseling, learning to help women with sexual abuse and eating disorder issues.

As an undergraduate, Bakke encountered many female athletes with body image problems. Today, she lives in Hawaii where her swimming skills help bring patients into therapeutic contact with wild dolphins in the ocean.

Are Swimmers Smarter Than Other Athletes?
> *"Swimmers have almost no fear. They walk around half naked for most of their lives."*
> — John Hargis

Pride in Identity

> *"When asked to give five things that you are (father, husband, businessman, etc.), I've always included 'swimmer' as one of mine. It's something I've always been proud of. It's given me a sense of purpose and achievement."*
> — Doug Martin

For Mike Barden, a sprint star at the Boys Club in the 1960s, pride in achievement came later in life. As a teenager and young adult, Barden said his swimming was ego-based and he was dismissive of others.

"Because I was fast, I was arrogant and thought I was special," Barden said. "I didn't give my competition and swimming buddies credit for what they had done for me."

After swimming at the University of Arkansas and coaching for several years, Barden came to understand himself better. "At 40, I started to look back. I realized a lot of things that kept me alive I had learned from Jimmy Miller and other coaches and swimmers."

Today, Barden is a message therapist and yoga teacher in Little Rock who has used his swimming skills to help people with disabilities improve water safety skills and health. He recalled the long-ago Boys Club swim team trips when, at Miller's

> *"At 40, I started to look back. I realized a lot of things that kept me alive I had learned from Jimmy Miller and other coaches and swimmers."*
> — Mike Barden

> "You have to be able to tap into yourself to be a great swimmer. The higher level you get to, the more you have to find out who you are and how to balance your life around swimming."
>
> Matt Twillie

request, he sat in the coveted passenger seat of the station wagon. On those trips, Miller treated him with friendship and respect, seeing in his fast young sprinter a maturity and character that Barden himself didn't recognize.

"Swimming does teach kids a lot about themselves, self-esteem, and purpose," Barden said. "Kids who are shy turn into team leaders. They open up and become better students because they can swim."

Hard work and work ethic

"Swimming drove home the understanding that if you work hard and are dedicated, you can accomplish anything. The work ethic, more than anything, is what I took from it."

Noel Strauss

"Swimming made a huge impact on the person I became," Autumn Buddenberg Taylor, an elementary school teacher for nearly thirty years, said. "I saw a direct connection between the effort put into a task and the quality of the outcome. Success or failure could not be placed on someone else's shoulders."

Taylor said competitive swimming and her teammate's hard work encouraged her to become personally responsible. The former Dolphins swimmer listed the skills she imparts to her students today, qualities such as goal setting, task completion, and time management. For Taylor, swimming was the classroom in which she learned those valuable life lessons.

Swimmers learn how achievement results from hard work. They also learn how to deal with disappointment and hardships.

"Swimmers have the daily opportunity to define their priorities, set and achieve goals, and gain a sense of accomplishment," Amy Gruber Burgess said. "These are key things that go a long way for any person in life."

"The training teaches you about work ethic. Swimming is an individual sport, so you are constantly challenging yourself to get better. Your nemesis is the clock, not anybody else. It's how fast you can go and only you can control that."

Rick Witherspoon

Abstract Concepts, Real Results

For many, a college scholarship is the most tangible benefit of age group swimming. For YWCA swimmer Jan Diner Hildebrandt, however, attending college was only the beginning.

As a freshman at Vanderbilt University, Hildebrandt was disappointed to learn the school had no women's swimming team. After years of age group and high school athletic success, Hildebrandt was not lacking in self confidence. She took action in the most direct manner she thought possible.

"We hired a student from the Vanderbilt Law School and filed suit under Title IX to establish a team," she said. "We never had to go to court. The school appointed an athletic director and created a women's team. We got suits, warms up, and other items. I even received a small athletic scholarship."

Matt Twillie, a Dolphins butterfly star in the 1980s, said swimming helped him maintain a balance in life among his physical, mental, and spiritual qualities. He believes the sport cultivates a holistic sense of self.

"You have to be able to tap into yourself to be a great swimmer," Twillie said. "The higher level you get to, the more you have to find out who you are and how to balance your life around swimming."

For Twillie, the lessons of winning and losing have enlarged his world experience and strengthened him to face life's challenges. David Guthrie agrees that competition produces strength of character, but he views competition as an artificial drama.

"I still get nervous when I first get to Masters Nationals, as if something really is

---

What is the Difference Between Sprinters and Distance Swimmers?
"Sprinters are lazy, and long distance swimmers have gigantic chips on their shoulders because the only races they can win are the ones no one else wants to suit up for."
Manning Field

at stake," Guthrie said. "When we put ourselves in fearful conditions and then overcome them, we get benefit without real consequences. It's all about growth and putting yourself under pressure. I learn from those experiences how to maintain a posture of facing adversity. Outside of swimming is where those lessons pay off."

"You learn how to get up and get going first thing in the morning. The discipline I learned as a swimmer taught me to stick with any corporate challenge. As a female professional in the 1980s working in technology and financial consulting, I've had no problem working with men my whole life. The social climate is huge in how swimmers learn to deal with members of the opposite sex."
— Anita Heil Parisi

Passing on the Passion

"The success I've had in life is a direct result of the people who invested in me with their time, love, and support. My success is due to people giving back. Swimming is the key to that for me."
— Larry Golden

Swim coaches and former Dolphins swimmers Tay Stratton and John Hargis strive to pass on to their athletes a passion for excellence, for applying themselves to the fullest extent possible, no matter the outcome.

Are Swimmers Smarter Than Other Athletes?
"It's not that swimmers are smarter, but they are forced to organize their time for training. Swimming is an educational tool to prioritize and organize your time."
— **Basil Hicks**

But a larger message accompanies the coaching process, Stratton said. "One of my main motivating forces is to teach them to never limit themselves, to push through to the freedom a true athlete has."

Hargis takes daily inspiration from his former age group coaches, Bob Courtway and Paul Blair. Their photos on his office wall, Hargis said, "take me back to where I've come from and what I need to do on a daily basis."

For Hargis, those Arkansas memories help him establish meaningful relations with his college swimmers.

"I have expectations for their success in life," Hargis said. "When a student says 'thank you for forcing me to go to class,' I've created something that will last much longer than the few years he'll be swimming. Take a kid you didn't think had a chance and watch him receive his degree, that brings me joy."

> "When we put ourselves in fearful conditions and then overcome them, we get benefit without real consequences. It's all about growth and putting yourself under pressure."
> — David Guthrie

Chapter 14. Afterword

On most weekday afternoons, a familiar scenario occurs at entrances of central Arkansas swimming pools. Car doors fly open and children of all ages spill out. A few may pause to say, "Thanks, Mom," before running to the building, backpacks cluttered with dolls, ribbons, and beads. Teenagers emerge with cell phones pressed to their ears. Too cool to rush, they drift inside at a leisurely pace, their attention focused only on keying in text messages or sharing with Facebook friends.

Within a few minutes, teens and preteens alike are on the pool deck. The coach explains the opening set. Non-attentive and late swimmers are chided. The coach explains the opening set again. Someone asks to go to the bathroom.

> **Are Swimmers Smarter Than Other Athletes?**
> "Swimming sharpened my ability to think about many things at once. It would amaze me how many things I could think about while I was in a race: hand and body position, breathing patterns, how to approach the wall. It was like a computer running so fast in your head."
> **Mike Barden**

Others excitedly share stories from school. A few have already dived in and begun the warm up. The coach points out those leadership skills to the stragglers and explains the opening set a final time. Eventually, all swimmers are moving down their assigned lanes, and for a few moments the only sound is of splashing water.

This is age group swimming's daily renewal, a process begun in Arkansas more than eighty years ago in the Little Rock YMCA and Boys Club basement pools.

A Turning Point

A turning point in the evolution of competitive swimming in central Arkansas took place in the 1960s. The entrepreneurial vision of two Arkansans—Jimmy Miller and Pat Riley, Sr.—brought Arkansas pools, coaches, and training into the modern era.

Miller Swim Gym is gone, but the Little Rock Racquet Club has endured. Despite four decades of changes, the club's central creed of producing world class athletes continues. Riley, now 87, sees a direct relation between family participation and athletic success.

"If you raise your children in a good atmosphere and put them into the type of sports that require real dedication and

> **What is the Difference Between Sprinters and Distance Swimmers?**
> "They are two different breeds of people. Sprinters are slackers. Distance swimmers are hard working and determined. You do a lot more strategy for the distance race. It's more of an art than a sprint."
> **Hannah Bakke**

sacrifice and highly competitive offerings, you have a chance to end up with a better adult. Today, many swimmers who were on the team years ago now work out at our club and are in excellent physical shape."

"When we first began, everybody was talking about programs for juniors. Then adults began to participate. Now with all the offerings, we have a true family club. We have great trainers and coaches who clue in to the old creed that competitive athletics leads to excellence in the sport as well as in life."

A Changing Role

Today, overall administration of the Racquet Club and other fitness facilities is the responsibility of Pat Riley, Jr. The

> "If you raise your children in a good atmosphere and put them into the type of sports that require real dedication and sacrifice and highly competitive offerings, you have a chance to end up with a better adult."
>
> Pat Riley, Sr.

> "Arkansas is still a basketball and football state, but I'm amazed at how many swimmers there are in Arkansas now."
>
> Noel Strauss

former Dolphins swimmer acknowledges changes in the nature of the club and its sponsorship role in swimming.

"When I was a swimmer in 1970, the club had about 500 members and 100 team swimmers," Riley said. "Now, we have more than 1,400 club members and an expanded team with swimmers on multiple levels. Adult lap swim, water aerobics, and Masters workouts are now part of the mix."

The Dolphin-Laser Swim team now requires several pools for its varied activities and seasonal needs. Summer training at the Racquet Club 50-meter pool is balanced with indoor workouts at UALR. Learn-to-swim and team development programs are conducted at several sites, including satellite locations in other Arkansas cities.

"The program is stronger than ever," Riley said. "The team has more coaches, more pools, and kids can swim at better times for their families. It's exciting to see summer league programs becoming more structured and Masters swimming developing and engaging triathletes."

The Next Wave of Growth

Some speculate that the next wave of Arkansas' swimming growth will occur in the booming northwest region of the state where Wal-Mart and other corporations have fueled a strong economy and created new upscale communities. The urban growth patterns Little Rock experienced in the 1960s are being repeated there.

Passing on the Torch
Blair Bish is congratulated by Tom Genz for breaking his 30-year old LSC record in the 100-Yard Breaststroke. Bish, 14, won the event with a 59.80 at the Arkansas State Championship meet in March 2011.

"Arkansas is still a basketball and football state," Noel Strauss said, "but I'm amazed at how many swimmers there are in Arkansas now."

Riley, who has inherited his father's passion for engaging adults and children in healthy activity, believes swimming's success and future is a result of its essential appeal to families. He sees a repeating pattern of families enrolling their children in swim classes, team development programs, and age group competitions.

"The most promising sign of all is that we are attracting second and third generations of swim families," he said.

What is the Difference Between Sprinters and Distance Swimmers?
"As Rocky Balboa said, 'If I could sing or dance, I wouldn't be a boxer.' Well, if you can sprint, you won't be a distance swimmer."

Pat Riley, Jr.

Appendices

Appendix A: Swim Teams and Head Coaches

Little Rock Racquet Club Dolphins/Little Rock Arkansas Dolphins
Audris Zidermanis
John Hays
Kees Oudegeest
Bob Teichart
Robbin White
Sam Freas
Paul Blair
Keith McAfee
John Hargis
Matt Adams
Basil Hicks

Little Rock Athletic Club Lasers
Tay Stratton
Matt Twillie

Miller Swim Gym
Jimmy Miller
Glenn Schultz
Sammy Turner
Mike Barden

Little Rock Boys Club—MEN
L. B. Parker
Edward Smith
Jimmy Miller
John Torbett
John Brooks
Jud Bryan

Little Rock Boys Club—WOMEN
Bess Butler
Edith Frazier

North Little Rock Boys Club
Ed Walker

South End Boys Club/ Thrasher Boys Club
Luther Armstrong

Little Rock YMCA
Jack Rusk
Miles Donoho
John Hays
John Brooks
Sammy Turner
Kahki Muren

Little Rock YWCA
Mary Lou Jaworski
Jan Marek
Mary Oudegeest
Els Strickland
John Brooks

Central Arkansas Swim Team
John Torbett
Richard Turner
Rusty Wright
Mary Oudegeest
Kellie Stratton
Matt Torbett
Angela Oudegeest

University of Arkansas at Little Rock
John Torbett
Richard Turner
Paul Blair
John Hargis
Amy Burgess
Matt Adams

Appendix B: Arkansans in 1969 National Age Group Top 5 Ranking

AAU NATIONAL TOP 5 AGE GROUP RANKINGS—20-Yard Pool
December 29, 1969, *Arkansas Gazette*

Age Group	Club	Swimmer	Event	Time	Ranking
15-17 Boys	LRRC	Pat Miles	500 Free	04:51.2	1st—national record
			200 Back	02:10.9	1st
			200 Free	01:51.5	3rd
			200 Fly	02:17.8	4th
	LRBC	David Adams	200 Fly	02:17.8	4th
		Sammy Turner	100 Free	51.5	5th
		Morgan Knox	500 Free	05:23.5	4th
		Chuck Nestrud	200 Breast	02:25.2	4th
		Paul Blair, Chuck Letzig, Sha Williamson, Chuck Nestrud	160 Free Relay	01:13.4	3rd
	Hendrix Aqua Kids	John Bumpers	100 back	59.4	5th
15-17 Girls	LRBC	Marc Bryan	100 Fly	01:06.7	5th
		Marc Bryan, Debbie Dunlop, Val Calhoun, Susan Letzig	160 Medley Relay	01:38.3	4th
		Hazel Thomas, Carrie Thomas, [?] Riley, [?] Snider	160 Medley Relay	01:38.6	5th
		Cathy Sunderland	100 Free	57.2	1st
			200 Back	02:34.0	4th
			100 Fly	01:04.9	3rd
	LR YWCA	Wendy Rynning	200 Fly	02:42.1	4th
		Cathy Sunderland, Wendy Rynning, Carol Davis, Margaret Bost	160 Free Relay	01:27.7	4th
13-14 Girls	LRBC	Melissa Thompson	100 Free	58.4	5th

Appendix B: Arkansans in 1969 National Age Group Top 5 Ranking (Continued)

Age Group	Club	Swimmer	Event	Time	Ranking
11-12 Boys	LRBC	Jim Bryan	100 Fly	01:11.8	2nd
		Mike Adams	100 Free	58.9	5th
			200 Free	02:14.7	1st
11-12 Girls	LRBC	Diane Letzig	100 Back	01:11.9	2nd
			200 Free	01:19.0	5th
10-Under Boys	LRBC	Ricky Witherspoon	200 Free	02:29.8	4th
			40 Back	27.4	5th
			100 Back	01:19.0	3rd
			160 IM	02:13.2	2nd
		Ricky Witherspoon, Bob Martin, Jim Handloser, Jeff O'Neal	160 Medley Relay	01:48.4	3rd
		Ricky Witherspoon, Bob Martin, Jim Handloser, Edward Lile	160 Free Relay	01:35.9	2nd
	LRRC	Trip Strauss	200 Free	02:26.9	3rd
		Jim Flack	[Event not listed]	01:20.2	4th
		David Gatchell	100 Fly	01:20.6	4th
10-Under Girls	LRBC	Susan Brooks	160 IM	02:20.9	4th
	LR YWCA	Karen Lamb	160 IM	02:19.3	3rd
	Miller Swim Gym	Laura Miller	200 Free	02:43.0	5th
			100 Back	01:26.6	3rd
			100 Fly	01:26.0	2nd

Appendix C: Arkansas Swimming Hall of Fame

The Arkansas Swimming Hall of Fame was conceived by Jerry Heil to recognize outstanding individuals and their contributions to swimming in Arkansas. The program was initiated by Paul Blair and a broad group of swimming advocates and supporters. The Arkansas Swimming Hall of Fame annually contributes funds to help the state's top swimmers participate in regional and national meets.

Arkansas Swimming Hall of Fame Inductees

1986	John Brooks, Jud Bryan, Bob Courtway, Pat Miles, Keena Rothhammer Weisbly, Jimmy Miller, Pat Riley, Sr.
1987	Linda Frazier Bland, John F. Torbett, Mary Lou Jaworski, Frank W. Letzig
1988	Jack Deacon, Randy Ensminger, Doug Martin
1989	Edith Frazier, Roy Gean, Karen Hight Russell, Kees Oudegeest, Bill Rogers
1990	Sam Freas, Harry Leggett, Jr., Pat Riley, Jr., Sammy Turner, Diane Letzig McDaniel
1991	Ed Fedosky, Clyde Brooks, Bill Stafford, Jerry Heil
1992	Paul Blair, John T. Bumpers, Edith Lynn Frazier, Roy Gean, III, J. Tom Welch
1993	John R. Hays, Tom Genz, Barry Deacon, John Garrett, Edward G. Smith
1994	Ollie W. Gatchell, Carl Quaintance, Mark Strauss, Richard Turner, Melissa Thompson
1995	Ronald Bank, John Donaldson, Paul Ladue, Coak Matthews, Mike Neuhofel
1996	Mary Heil, Cathy Snider Brewton, Martin Smith
1997	Carolyn Haefner, Grover Evans, Jon Olsen, Tom Roberts, Jeff Davis
1998	Mickey Gunn, Eric J. Heil, William Terry
1999	Anita A. Harrison, Marvin Schwartz
2000	Thomas W. Jones, Noel Strauss, Matt Twillie
2001	William James Dann, John Hargis, Richard Kersh, Marybeth Heil Rosell
2002	Wesley Clark, Steve Claycomb, Kellie Stratton Coleman, Bud Jackson
2003	Mary Kay Fitzgerald, David Gean, Harvey Humphries, Trip Strauss
2004	Mike Booth, Neil Bradley, Nancy Duncan, Sande Southerland
2005	Scott C. Claycomb, Judy Smith Pannier, Bob Staab
2006	David Gillanders, David Guthrie, Greg Magness, Anita Parisi
2007	Basil Hicks, Jim Kelly, Tay Stratton
2008	Liz Genz, Larry Golden, Sue Wrape
2009	Tom Gean, Keith McAfee, Mindy Matheny Giraudeau
2010	Neka Mabry, Mary Dawn Blair

Biographies of all Arkansas Swimming Hall of Fame inductees are available on the Arkansas Swimming Inc. website.

Appendix D: Dolphins Achievements

Note: Listings were compiled from local swim team records and may not be fully inclusive of all swimmers and achievements.

LRRC National Age Group Champions

Year		Swimmer	Age	Event
1989	SC	Basil Hicks	13-14	500 Freestyle
	SC	Noel Strauss	15-16	100 Freestyle
	SC	Matt Twillie	15-16	100 Butterfly
1988	SC	Noel Strauss	15-16	100 Freestyle
	SC	Matt Twillie	15-16	100 Butterfly
	LC	Noel Strauss	15-16	50, 100 Freestyle
1987	LC	Noel Strauss	13-14	50, 100, 200 Meter Freestyle
				200 Free Relay
	SC	Noel Strauss	13-14	50,100 Freestyle
	SC	Matt Twillie	13-14	100 Butterfly
1986	LC	Noel Strauss	13-14	50, 100 Freestyle
1985	LC	Noel Strauss	11-12	50, 100 Freestyle
	LC	Mike Neuhofel	17-18	50 Freestyle
	SC	Mike Neuhofel	17-18	50 Freestyle
1984	LC	Tom Genz	17-18	100 Breaststroke
1983	LC	Tom Genz	17-18	100, 200 Breaststroke
	SC	Tom Genz	17-18	100, 200 Breaststroke, 200 IM
1982	LC	Tom Genz	15-16	100 Breaststroke
	SC	Tom Genz	15-16	100, 200 Breaststroke, 200 IM
1981	SC	Tom Genz	13-14	100 Freestyle, 200 IM

1990 Top 16

Swimmer	Age	Rank	Event	Time
Basil Hicks	15	16th	1650 Yards Freestyle	15:47.22
Manning Field	16	11th	200 Yard Breaststroke	2:05.88
Matt Twillie	18	2nd	100 Yard Butterfly	48.79
Noel Strauss	17	14th	50 Yard Freestyle	20.84
		9th	100 Yard Freestyle	45.24
		12th	200 Yard Freestyle	1:39.24

1995 Top 16

Swimmer	Age	Rank	Event	Time
Chris Sheppard	15-16	15th	200 Meter Backstroke	2:09.74
Daniel Pupkowski	10 & U	12th	50 Meter Butterfly	33.42
Hannah Bakke	10 & U	8th	100 Meter Breaststroke	1:26.19
		8th	50 Meter Breaststroke	39.18
John Hicks	13-14	12th	1000 Yard Freestyle	9:46.37
		8th	1500 Meter Freestyle	16:37.54
		4th	1650 Yard Freestyle	16:07.67
		6th	400 Meter Freestyle	4:12.83
		14th	800 Meter Freestyle	8:45.99

Dolphin-Laser Top 10 National Age Group Ranking since 2007

Swimmer	Age	Year	Event	National Rank
Jordan Sweet	10	2009	100-Meter Breaststroke	6th
	9	2008	200-Yard Breaststroke	6th
Jessie Garrison	13	2009	800-Meter Freestyle	1st
	13	2009	200-Meter Butterfly	2nd
Delaney Haralson	10	2009	200-Meter Butterfly	9th
	10	2009	1500 -Meter Freestyle	4th
Tim Barnett	12	2007	1500 -Meter Freestyle	6th
Olivia Keith	9	2010	50-Meter Breaststroke	9th
Ravi Sun	14	2009	200-Meter backstroke	7th
Shelby Burleson	12	2009	1500-Meter Freestyle	10th

Appendix D: Dolphins Achievements (Continued)

Paul Blair and Dolphins Swim Team Achievements

Blair served on the Olympic International Operations Committee and was Vice-President of the American Swim Coaches Association. He served as the Head Coach for the USA World Championship team and National Junior Team Youth Olympic Festival. He was a Nike Advisory Coach and USA National Team Coach.

Blair became a member of Liberty State College's Hall of Fame in 1991 and the Arkansas Swimming Hall of Fame in 1992. In 2004, he received the World Swimming Coaches Association Yutaka Terao Award. He was posthumously inducted into the American Swimming Coaches Association (ASCA) Coaches Hall of Fame.

Blair served on various state and national boards including being Vice-President of the American Swim Coaches Association, International Swimming Hall of Fame Board of Governors, and the State of Arkansas Governor's Council for Sport and Fitness.

Individual Achievements

- 8 time USA National Team Coach
- 6 US National Champions
- 1 US Open National Champion
- 12 Junior National Champions
- 2 Olympic Festival Gold Medalists
- 35 National Age Group Champions
- 17 National Age Group Records
- 7 Masters National Champions
- 1 Pan American Silver Medalist
- 25 World Ranked Swimmers
- 25 Olympic Trials Qualifiers
- 4 Pan Pacific Team Members
- 6 Olympic Swimmers
- 1 World Team Silver Medalist
- 1 Olympic Gold Medalist

Team Championships

- 1988 US Open Men's Team Champions
- 1989 US Men's Team National Champions
- 10 time Region VIII Team Champions
- 57 Arkansas State Age Group Championships

1990   6th place Men's Team—US Nationals (sc)
Coach of Doug Boyd, 4th in world, 50 Meter Freestyle

1989   1st place Men's Team—US Nationals (sc)
Coach of Steve Crocker, 2nd in world, 50 Meter Freestyle
Region 8 Coach of the Year (sc)

1988   1st place Men's Team—US Open
Coach of 3 US Nationals' finalists—Crocker, Genz, Strauss
11 Olympic Trial Qualifiers
3 swimmers ranked Top 25 in the world

1987   Arkansas Swimming Inc. Coach of the Year
      Nominated—US Coach of the Year
      13th place at US Nationals (sc)
Coach:
      Noel Strauss, 5 National Age Group records & Junior Olympic champion
      Neil Bradley—Senior National finalist, 100 Backstroke
      Tom Genz—Senior National finalist, 100 Breaststroke
      Mike Neuhofel—Pan Am silver medal, 50 Freestyle
      Mindy Matheny—Senior National finalist, 50 Freestyle

Appendix D: Dolphins Achievements (Continued)

1986 Arkansas Swimming Inc. Coach of the Year
    Nominated—US Coach Of Year
    4th place Men's Team—US Nationals (sc)
Coach:
    Tom Genz—1st at US Senior Nationals,
    100 Breaststroke
    Noel Strauss—1st at US Junior Olympics, 50 Freestyle
    Mike Neuhofel—Finalist at Senior Nationals,
    50 Freestyle

1985 Arkansas Swimming Inc. Coach of the Year
    Nominated—US Coach Of Year
Coach:
    Genz, Neuhofel, Anita Harrison (Senior National finalists)
    Asst Coach: USA team @ USS international meet

1984 Eric Heil—1st place at Junior Olympics, 400 Freestyle
1983 Tom Genz—First LRRC swimmer with world ranking
1982 Tom Genz—1st place at Junior Olympics, 100 Breaststroke

Index

1956 Olympics at Melbourne 14, 56
1976 Olympics at Montreal 14
1980 Olympics at Moscow 57
1996 Olympics at Atlanta 92, 93
Adams, David 128
Adams, Lisa 43
Adams, Matt 102, 106, 108, 110, 127
Adams, Mike 129
Alcatraz Sharkfest Swim 113
Allen, Gail 44
American Swim Coaches Association 132
American Swimming Coaches Association Hall of Fame 132
Arkansas AAU swimming 17, 18, 25, 26, 27, 29, 31, 35, 57, 59
Arkansas Democrat 6, 14, 20, 22, 28, 33, 35, 39, 47, 55, 56, 57, 58, 75, 76, 88
Arkansas Democrat-Gazette 9, 20
Arkansas Gazette 21, 23, 24, 25, 27, 28, 29, 33, 35, 38, 41, 43, 44, 47, 60, 61, 73, 74, 75, 78, 80, 82, 86, 107, 128
Arkansas Governor's Council for Sport and Fitness 132
Arkansas High School State Championships 28
Arkansas Junior Olympic 35, 43
Arkansas Louisiana Gas Company 51
Arkansas Masters Swimming 7, 35, 57, 113, 114, 115, 116, 117
Arkansas School for the Blind 25
Arkansas Swimming Hall of Fame 16, 25, 26, 29, 34, 65, 66, 68, 73, 78, 130, 132, 141
Arkansas Symphony Orchestra 80
Arkansas Travelers 39
Armstrong, Luther 127

Ashe, Arthur 50, 52
Atlantic City Steel Pier 33
Auburn University 93
Bailey, Dr. and Mrs. Ted 50
Bakke, Hannah 9, 88, 98, 99, 103, 119, 123, 131
Baldwin & Shell Construction 29
Bank, Kay 114
Bank, Ron 113, 114, 130
Barden, Mike 38, 119, 123, 127
Barham, Mark 103
Barnett, Tim 104, 131
Bartlesville, Oklahoma 44, 61, 75
Barton, Johnny 31
Bass, Patrick 9, 106, 109
Bell, Alvin 19
Bell, Bobby 22
Benkovitz, Ann 44
Berkhoff, David 77
Berry, John 103
Biondi, Matt 98
Bish, Blair 124
Blair, Lindann 88
Blair, Mary Dawn 9, 91, 92, 130
Blair, Paul 13, 16, 64, 67, 71, 72, 73, 74, 75, 77, 78, 79, 80, 81, 84, 85, 86, 90, 91, 92, 94, 98, 99, 101, 102, 104, 106, 107, 108, 117, 121, 127, 128, 130, 132
Blair, Shawna 88
Bland, Linda Frazier 41, 53, 54, 56, 57, 58, 59, 60, 63, 87, 130
Bogart, Eleanor 28
Bonds, John 55
Booth, Mike 9, 73, 75, 130
Borchert, Martin 51

Bost, Margaret 43, 128
Bowen, Patty 43
Bowen, Scott 63
Boyd, Doug 77, 82, 84, 85, 99, 132
Bradley, Greg 73
Bradley, Neil 75, 76, 81, 82, 130, 132
Branch, Bobby 22, 24, 31
Branch, Jack 22, 24, 25
Brann, Mary Oudegeest 55, 56, 57, 72, 113, 127
Brewton, Cathy Snider 130
Britt, Lt. Governor Maurice "Footsie" 51
Brockman, Oliver 20
Brooke, Robert 27
Brooks Pool Company 25
Brooks, Clyde 36, 40, 41, 42, 44, 130
Brooks, John 9, 23, 24, 47, 65, 113, 127, 130
Brooks, Susan 43, 129
Bryan, Jim 110, 129
Bryan, Jud 47, 65, 127, 130
Bryan, Marc (see Perrine, Marc Ann Bryan)
Bubble Babble 58
Bumpers, Governor Dale 63
Bumpers, John 128, 130
Burch, Coy 22
Burgess, Amy Gruber 21, 87, 90, 94, 98, 102, 106, 120, 127
Burleson, Shelby 104, 109, 131
Burris, Mickey 35, 100
Burris, Sandy 6
Burton, Mike 58
Butler, Bess 21, 24, 27, 28, 29, 34, 127
Caddo River 28
Calhoun, Val 128
Callaway, Clell 67

Camp Aldersgate 29
Camp Matthews 24
Camp Robinson 27
Campbell, Robinson 20
Carmichael, Ritchie 36
Carmichael, Rod 36
Carson, Flora 20
Casey, Sean 91, 98
Catholic High School 38, 65, 78
Caulkins, Tracy 64
Central Arkansas Swim Club 9, 80, 106, 109
Central Arkansas Swim League 73
Central Arkansas Swim Team 57, 71, 72, 73, 76, 88, 127
Central High School 31, 87, 88, 89, 90, 111
Cipriani, Barney 24
Clark, Wesley 35, 37, 45, 130
Claycomb, Scott 76, 78, 130
Claycomb, Steve 75, 76, 130
Clinton, President Bill 94
Collins, Ryan 36
Conway Aqua Kids 80
Conway High School 99
Conway, Arkansas 11, 19, 24, 29, 33, 44, 68, 76, 80, 82, 92
Cook, Ferris 6
Corden, Marvin 22
Coulter, Murray 28
Countryman, Buddy 25
Courtway, Bob 80, 92, 121, 130
Cox, Aaron 108, 111, 112
Cox, Shelby 108
Craighead, Thomas 21
Crawford, Gene 22, 24, 27, 28
Crocker, Steve 77, 82, 84, 85, 99, 106, 132
Dann, William James 130
Davis, Carol 128
Davis, Jeff 50, 130
Deacon, Barry 130
Deacon, Jack 130

Diemer, Elmer 23
Dill, Dorothy 20
Dischinger, Drew 103
Dixon, Keith 117
Dolan, Kevin 36, 40, 42
Dolphin-Laser Swim Team 79, 98, 101, 102, 103, 104, 106, 108, 109, 111, 124, 131
Donaldson, John 130
Donoho, Doug 36, 40, 42
Donoho, Miles 40, 127
Dover High School 74
Dover YMCA 74
Dover, Ohio 74
Driver, Charles 20
Duncan, Nancy 82, 130, 138
Dunlop, Debbie 128
East St. Louis YMCA 55
Eichler, Brad 116
El Dorado, Arkansas 23, 25, 109
English Channel 56, 57
Ensminger, Glenda 65
Ensminger, Randy 9, 57, 65, 66, 78, 130
Esentan, Troy 108
ESPN 81
Evans, Grover 130
Fair Park Pool 19, 20, 24, 26, 28, 29, 33
Fayetteville Youth Center 57
Fedosky, Ed 130
Field, Manning 67, 87, 92, 120, 131
Field, Rick 91, 113, 115
fire dive 17, 19, 20
First National Bank 50
Fitzgerald, Mary Kay 130
Fitzgibbon, Henry 22
Flack, Jim 129
Flannigan, John 118
Flatbush Boys Club 21
Fleenor, Ricky 36, 40, 41, 42, 44
Forest Park 18
Fort Smith Tideriders 76

Fort Smith, Arkansas 11, 19, 31, 33, 46, 114
Frazier, Edith 34, 35, 39, 40, 41, 51, 127, 130
Frazier, Edith Lynn 41, 44, 130
Freas, Sam 64, 65, 66, 74, 84, 107, 127, 130
Freeman, J. J. 50
Fryer, Wally 25
Fulbright, Senator J. William 63
Gambrill, Don 59
Garner, Gilbert 23
Garrett, John 81, 130
Garrison, Jessie 104, 108, 109, 131
Gary Schultz Memorial Award 80
Gassaway, Debbie 44
Gaston, Jack 25
Gatchell, Caroline 50
Gatchell, Chip 44
Gatchell, David 129
Gatchell, Oliver "Ollie" 49, 50, 53, 55, 130
Gattini, Sandra 76, 81
Gean, David 76, 130
Gean, Roy 76, 130
Gean, III, Roy 130
Gean, Tom 130
Gentry, Roy 9, 28, 29
Genz, Liz 67, 68, 70, 79, 130
Genz, Terry 9, 68
Genz, Tom 71, 72, 73, 74, 75, 76, 78, 80, 82, 84, 99, 106, 110, 124, 130, 131, 132, 133
George Washington University 118
Gillam Park 31
Gillanders, David 114, 130
Ginocchio-Cromwell and Associates 50
Glover, Natalie 58
Goldberg, Harriet 28
Golden, Larry 71, 75, 102, 115, 121, 130
Gore, Karen 11
Grall, Tom 107
Green, Charles 28
Grimes, Brenda 6
Gruenberg, Billy 21

Gruenberg, Paul 20, 21
Gunn, Hamilton 17
Gunn, Jackie 25
Gunn, Mickey 22, 24, 25, 28, 29, 37, 130
Guthrie, David 90, 91, 107, 116, 120, 121, 130
Haefner, Carolyn 130
Hall High School 59, 99, 108
Handloser, Jim 44, 129
Haralson, Delaney 104, 131
Harding, Betsy 88, 90
Hargis, John 87, 92, 93, 94, 97, 101, 103, 105, 106, 119, 121, 127, 130
Hargis, Sonny 92, 94
Harrison, Anita A. (see Henry, Anita Harrison)
Harvard Business School 49
Hays, John 45, 51, 52, 127, 130
Heights 18
Heil Mile Award 68
Heil, Becky 67
Heil, Eric 70, 73, 75, 81, 82, 130, 133
Heil, Jerry 55, 68, 130
Heil, Mary 68, 70, 130
Henderson State University 109
Hendrix AAU Invitational at Conway 44
Hendrix College 33, 41, 55, 80, 92, 100, 116
Hendrix Pentathlon 114
Henry, Anita Harrison 76, 80, 94, 130, 133
Henry, Orville 60, 61
Heye, Trey 108, 110, 111
Hicks, Barbara 11
Hicks, Basil 53, 84, 88, 90, 92, 97, 98, 99, 104, 106, 121, 127, 130, 131
Hicks, John 88, 91, 98, 131
High School All-American 66, 103
Hight, Karen 58, 62, 130
Hildebrandt, Jan Diner 34, 35, 43, 100, 101, 120
Hiller, Ann 94
Hlavacek, Ida 114
Hoff, Sonny 22, 24
Hogan, Jacque 28

Holt, Katheryn 88
Hot Springs National Park 33
Humphries, Harvey 14, 36, 37, 44, 95, 100, 102, 130
Humphries, Sara Kay 37, 101
Indiana University 67, 82, 87, 101
International Swimming Hall of Fame 4, 56, 107, 132
Jackson, Bud 114, 115, 130
Jager, Tom 83, 93
James, Obell 23
James, Odell 23
Jaworski, Mary Lou 9, 11, 31, 34, 35, 40, 43, 100, 101, 113, 127, 130
Jennings Lake 29
Jennings, Alston 21
John Brown University 55
Johnson, Jim 114, 115
Jones, Priscilla 87, 89, 92, 94
Jones, Thomas W. 130
Jonesboro, Arkansas 11, 19, 33, 49, 76
Junior Olympics 35, 43, 101, 133
Junior Swimmer magazine 42
Justings, Bo 25
Kavanaugh Boulevard 18
Keith, Helen 14
Keith, Olivia 104, 131
Kelly, Jim 130
Kenchilo, Zelma 20
Kennedy, Edward 20
Kersh, Richard 130
Kincannon, Jay 44
Kindl, Brian 92
Kirchner, Ken 64
Kletzel, Jonathan 87, 89, 90, 92
Knot Hole Gang 39
Knox, Morgan 128
Koonce, Tony 24, 25, 26, 28, 29
Korean War 29
Kramer, Billy 17

Kramer, Rosalind 17, 22, 24, 27
Kramer, Ruth 17, 22
Ladue, Paul 130
Lafferty, Peggy 28
Lamb, Karen 129
Leggett, Jr., Harry 130
Letzig, Chuck 9, 128
Letzig, Diane 6, 43, 45, 58, 59, 129, 130
Letzig, Frank 34, 52, 68, 130
Letzig, Kathy 43
Lile, Edward 44, 129
Linsley Military Institute 74
Little Maumelle River 23, 37
Little Rock Athletic Club 73, 94, 106, 127
Little Rock Boys Club 13, 14, 15, 17, 20, 21, 22, 23, 24, 25, 26, 27, 28, 29, 31, 33, 34, 35, 36, 37, 38, 39, 40, 41, 42, 44, 45, 46, 47, 49, 51, 52, 53, 54, 55, 57, 61, 65, 68, 71, 73, 101, 109, 113, 119, 123, 127
Little Rock High School 25, 38, 57
Little Rock Junior College 26, 28, 29, 47
Little Rock Kiwanis Club 23
Little Rock Lasers Swim Team 72, 95, 111
Little Rock Racquet Club 7, 16, 39, 49, 50, 51, 52, 53, 54, 55, 56, 57, 58, 59, 60, 64, 67, 68, 71, 72, 73, 74, 78, 79, 81, 87, 88, 93, 98, 100, 105, 106, 114, 116, 117, 123, 124, 127
Little Rock Recreation Commission 18
Little Rock YWCA 6, 11, 20, 23, 31, 33, 34, 35, 39, 43, 44, 45, 46, 49, 52, 57, 65, 71, 98, 100, 101, 114, 120, 127, 128
Little Rock/Arkansas Dolphins Swim Team 7, 13, 54, 57, 58, 60, 62, 63, 64, 65, 67, 68, 71, 72, 73, 74, 75, 76, 77, 78, 79, 80, 81, 82, 84, 85, 87, 88, 89, 90, 91, 92, 93, 94, 95, 97, 98, 99, 100, 102, 103, 104, 105, 106, 108, 110, 111, 112, 116, 117, 118, 119, 120, 121, 124, 127, 131, 132, 133
Lorge, Frank 115
Mabry, Neka 4, 9, 95, 103, 104, 110, 130

Maddox, Pat 14
Magness, Greg 130
Maguire, Michelle 90
Marak, Jan 44
Marek, Jan 127
Marquis de Sade Swim Meet 114
Marsh, David 93
Marshall, Amie 90
Martin, Bob 129
Martin, Doug 9, 44, 46, 51, 52, 53, 58, 78, 97, 99, 100, 115, 119, 130
Martin, Greg 40
Marus, J. J. 92, 102, 103, 105
Matheny, Mindy 76, 81, 82, 130, 132
Matthews, Charles 38, 113
Matthews, Coak 130
May, Harold 26, 28
McAfee, Keith 9, 74, 94, 104, 127, 130
McCarthy, Nick 99, 108
McCrary, Dave 82
McMath, Phil 36
McVey, Lindsey 87, 89, 92, 94
Meeks, Landon 107
Memphis Athletic Club 43
Memphis State University 76
Miles, E.C. 67
Miles, Pat 35, 44, 54, 57, 58, 78, 97, 128, 130
Miller Swim Gym 35, 36, 46, 47, 52, 55, 57, 61, 64, 65, 69, 88, 94, 95, 112, 123, 127, 129
Miller, Boonie 37, 46, 47, 60, 62, 67
Miller, Jimmy 13, 15, 22, 23, 25, 29, 35, 36, 37, 40, 44, 46, 47, 52, 55, 60, 61, 62, 65, 67, 68, 71, 79, 101, 108, 113, 119, 123, 127, 130
Miller, Laura 129
Millington Naval Base at Memphis 33, 41
Millwood Pool 17
Mitchell, Billy 21, 22, 35, 52
Monticello, Arkansas 27, 39
Moose, Bill 20
Mount St. Mary Academy 29

Muren, Kahki 127
Murphy, Shannon 107
Natchitoches, Louisiana 25
National AAU Swimming and Diving Championships 24, 26, 57
Neil Martin Victory Trophy 22, 25, 26, 28, 31, 65
Nelsen, Adam 94
Nelson, Debby 14
Nestrud, Chuck 128
Neuhofel, Mike 9, 68, 75, 76, 80, 81, 82, 84, 95, 98, 99, 130, 131, 132, 133
Norman, Kenyon 81
North Little Rock Boys Club 34, 109, 127
Northwestern Louisiana State College 25, 28, 33, 61
O'Bryan, Bobby 103
O'Neal, Jeff 129
Ohio University 74
Ohio Valley YMCA 74
Olsen, Jon 76, 130
Olson, Sam 99, 108
Olympic International Operations Committee 132
Otter Creek Swim Team 73
Ouachita Baptist University 103
Oudegeest, Angela 72, 127
Oudegeest, Kees 9, 54, 55, 56, 57, 58, 60, 62, 63, 91, 127, 130
Owen, Julie 14
Pan American Games 35, 54, 55, 57, 58, 80, 82
Pan Pacific Games 80
Para Olympics 11
Parisi, Anita Heil 68, 70, 108, 121, 130
Parker, L. B. 21, 35, 127
Parkview High School 72
Patton, Tom 107
Peavey, Paul 88, 105
Penick, Jr., James 50
Penn State University 93
Perrine, Marc Ann Bryan 35, 40, 52, 128

Peterson, Brent 88
Peterson, Chris 107
Pfeifer Kiwanis Camp 23, 37, 38
Pfeifer, Joseph 23
Pfeifer, Preston 23
Pfeiffer's Department Store 19
Phelps, Michael 103
Philips Oil Company 61
Phillips, Barnett 114
Piper, Virginia 22
Pirnique, Frank 44
Plemmons, Frank 36
Plemmons, Robert 36
Potter, Carolyn 22
Powell, Dan 82
Pryor, Governor David 62, 63
Pulaski Heights Junior High School 35
Pupkowski, Daniel 88, 103, 131
Quaintance, Carl 22, 24, 25, 26, 28, 130
Rainey, Robert 50
Rasnic, Lexi 4
Red Bridge Club 23, 37
Reese, Ed 64
Reigler, Eugene 23
Reinhart, Nicole 76, 81
Rheinhart, J.D. 20
Rice University 116
Riley, Martha 50
Riley, Sr., Pat 9, 49, 50, 51, 52, 54, 73, 123, 130
Riley, Jr., Pat 58, 63, 78, 88, 123, 124, 130
Roberts, J. B. 23
Roberts, Tom 26, 39, 130
Rockefeller, Governor Winthrop 50, 51
Roehrenbeck, Susan Letzig 100, 128
Rogers, Bill 130
Rosell, Marybeth Heil 130
Rothhammer, Keena 35, 45, 46, 59, 67, 75, 101, 130
Rouse, Jeff 93
Rusk, Jack 127

Ryan, Eimear 106, 108
Rynning, Wendy 11, 128
San Diego, California 24, 26, 28, 111
Santa Clara Swim Club 82
Santander, Carlos 105
Schienvar, Elaine 95
Schmand, Del 115
Schmidt, Richard 28
Schollander, Don 75, 83
Schultz, Gary 80, 112
Schultz, Glenn 127
Schwartz, Marvin 115, 116, 117, 130, 141
Scott, Leroy 19
Scott, Raymond 17
Senior Olympics 11
Shamrock Hotel 101
Shell, Bob 29
Sheppard, Chris 88, 131
Shojahee, Arianna 108
Shreveport East Ridge Country Club 44
Signoracci, John 23
Simmen, Charlotte 20
Sims, Bryan 67
Sisemore, Dick 25
Smith, Edward 127, 130
Smith, Judy 45, 130
Smith, Martin 66, 130
Smothers, Lee 109
Sonoja, Gustavo 63
South End Boys Club 31
Southeast Conference 93
Southerland, Ricky 75, 76, 81
Southerland, Sande 73, 75, 81, 130
Southern Illinois University 58
Southern Methodist University 54, 58, 78, 95
Southwest Conference 26, 49, 54, 64, 65, 81, 82
Southwest Times Record 31
Spanish National Minister of Sports 63
Spanish Swimming Federation 63
Special Olympics 11

Spencer, Jerry 57, 66
Spitz, Mark 83
Splash Racquet Club 49
Staab, Bob 74, 81, 82, 85, 130
Stafford, Bill 57, 64, 78, 130
Stahl, Ott C. 20
Stein, John 115
Stephens, Inc. 68
Stephens, Witt 50
Stevens, Walter 44
Stewart, Mike 38
Stiles, Sam 28
Stockton, Mark 44
Storey, Pat 17
Stratton, Kellie 67, 72, 127, 130
Stratton, Skye 100
Stratton, Tasha 106
Stratton, Tay 9, 72, 94, 95, 104, 106, 112, 121, 127, 130
Strauss, Mark 130
Strauss, Noel 53, 73, 81, 82, 83, 84, 85, 87, 91, 97, 98, 100, 120, 124, 130, 131, 132, 133
Strauss, Jr., Sam 49, 50
Strauss, Scott 90, 94
Strauss, Trip 78, 83, 86, 108, 117, 119, 129, 130
Strickland, Els 127
Sullivan, Kathy 40, 43, 57, 58, 59
Sun, Ravi 104, 109, 131
Sun, Ryland 108, 110
Sunderland, Cathy 128
Sweet, Jordan 104, 108, 131
SWIM Magazine 9, 116
Swimming World 84, 87, 98
Syracuse University 118
Taylor, Autumn Buddenberg 34, 58, 59, 98, 120
Teichart, Bob 64, 127
Terry, William 130
Texas A&M University 77
Thomas, Carrie 128
Thomas, Hardie 20, 22, 24, 33

Thomas, Hazel 128
Thomas, Jane 6
Thomas, Sherman 20
Thompson, Frank 22
Thompson, George 72
Thompson, Melissa 57, 128, 130
Thrasher Boys Club 31, 113, 127
Todd, Sandra 84
Torbett, John 47, 65, 71, 127, 130
Torbett, Matt 72, 127
Torrijo, Gustavo 76
Traindale, Ray 24
Tucker, Mary Grace 112
Tungac, Onat 109
Turner, Richard 44, 68, 91, 107, 110, 127, 130
Turner, Sammy 9, 33, 36, 40, 41, 42, 44, 100, 127, 128, 130
Twillie, Manuel 9
Twillie, Matt 31, 54, 72, 81, 84, 85, 87, 89, 90, 95, 100, 102, 106, 108, 120, 127, 130, 131
U.S. Davis Cup 50, 52
U.S. Olympic Committee 20
U.S. Olympic Training Center 87
United States Marine Corps 24, 111
United States Naval Academy 111
University of Alabama 59, 76, 80
University of Arkansas 29, 47, 49, 55, 57, 59, 64, 65, 66, 70, 71, 80, 82, 85, 119, 127, 141
University of Arkansas at Little Rock 29, 47, 59, 71, 72, 73, 79, 88, 94, 104, 106, 107, 108, 110, 124, 127
University of Georgia 95, 104
University of Illinois 31
University of Kansas 33
University of Kentucky 77
University of Missouri at Rolla 106
University of Nebraska 82
University of Texas 26, 64, 82
USA Today 81
Vanderbilt University 58, 120

Vencill, Kicker 103, 105, 106
Verona, Donna de 41
Vineyard, Gordon 35
Wafer, Marybeth 14
Wafer, Sandra 14
Wafer, Sara 14
Walker, Ed 127
Waller, Bernard 25
War Memorial Pool 19, 20, 32, 33, 37, 38, 41
Warren YMCA 20
Warren, Arkansas 19, 33, 43, 76
Weghorst, Matt 88, 90, 103, 105
Welch, J. Tom 130
West Liberty State College 74
West Little Rock Optimist Club 62, 68, 81, 88
West Little Rock YMCA 62
West Point 45
West Virginia 64, 74
West, George 42, 44
Western Kentucky State University 82, 106
Westside YMCA 88
White City Pool 17, 18, 19, 21, 23, 24
White, Robbin 62, 64, 78, 79, 127
Wilkes, Elbert 21
Williamson, Robert 36
Williamson, Sha 36, 41, 128
Willow Springs 17
Wilmoth, Brooks 99, 108
Wilson, Arkansas 33
Wilson, Jeff 38
Wilson, Kelly 90, 91
Wise, Benny 9, 33, 34, 35, 113
Withee, Allan 20
Witherspoon, Lawrence 51
Witherspoon, Rick 44, 54, 63, 100, 110, 120, 129
Womack, Mary Lou (see Jaworsky, Mary Lou)
World Swimming Coaches Association Yutaka Terao Award 132
World University Games 105, 106
Worthen Bank and Trust Company 50

WPA project 19
Wrape, Sue Keith 20, 22, 24, 28, 58, 97, 130
Wright, Rusty 71, 72, 127
Yale University 75, 104
Young, Luther 22
Zheng, Eric 99, 108
Zidermanis, Audris "Zeke" 51, 52, 127

About the Author

Marvin Schwartz is a Little Rock-based writer who specializes in biography and history. He has a Masters of Fine Arts in Poetry from the University of Arkansas. A former high school and college swimmer and a swim parent, he has been a Masters swimmer for nearly thirty years and has won seven Masters national championships. He was inducted into the Arkansas Swimming Hall of Fame in 1999.

Previously Published:

Arkansas History:
  Central in Our Lives
  Learning from the Land
  J.B. Hunt: The Long Haul to Success
  Tyson: From Farm to Market
  People of the Land
  Volunteers in Service to America: A History of VISTA in Arkansas

Poetry:
  Poems for a Temporal Body
  Passages

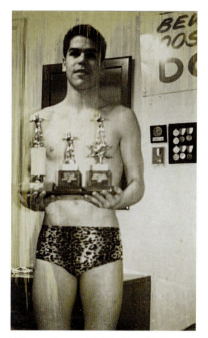

The author, with his first high school swim trophies, poses for a daring fashion statement, circa 1965.